ONLY ONE BAPTISM OF THE HOLY SPIRIT

ONLY ONE BAPTISM
of the Holy Spirit

PETER MASTERS

THE WAKEMAN TRUST * LONDON

**ONLY ONE BAPTISM
OF THE HOLY SPIRIT**

This edition first published 1994

THE WAKEMAN TRUST
5 Templar Street
London SE5 9JB

ISBN 1 870855 17 5

Cover design by Andrew Sides

Printed in Great Britain by The Alden Press, Oxford

Contents

1. When is a Believer Baptised With the Spirit?

THE VIEW THAT everyone who is converted to Christ needs a further baptism of the Spirit, or a 'second blessing', has been no more than a fringe teaching among evangelical Christians for over two centuries. In recent years, however, it has become a principal plank of the charismatic movement world-wide, and has even begun to penetrate conservative and reformed circles.

Most charismatic writers refer with disdain to 'traditional' evangelicals, whom they regard as third-rate Christians who proudly refuse to receive the fulness of the Spirit and the gift of tongues. They speak of 'hide-bound traditionalists'.

But where do charismatic teachers and those who share their views about the baptism of the Spirit get their ideas from? The answer, regrettably, is from people who approach the Bible in a shallow and careless manner, virtually ignoring the Bible's own rules of interpretation. The promoters of a baptism of the Spirit *after* conversion always pluck texts out of context and pay no attention to the fact that the vast majority of Bible passages *on the same subject* contradict their interpretations.

This was the complaint of a famous Bible teacher named William Biederwolf, who in 1913 protested about the many contradictory statements on the Holy Spirit which were made by some of the preachers in his day. He noticed that these statements, though dogmatic, were seldom supported by texts, and when they were, a mere glance at the text showed that it did not confirm the preachers' claims. Dr Biederwolf set himself the task of assembling all the Scripture references to different aspects of the work of the Spirit, and produced a book that stands today as a classic.*

The idea that Christians need a baptism of the Spirit after and in addition to their conversion is simply not borne out by the Bible. This chapter will take a look at all the texts which tell us *when* the believer is baptised with the Spirit. These texts will be quoted from the King James version, but readers are invited to check

---

**A Help to the Study of the Holy Spirit*, W. E. Biederwolf, Baker Book House (Grand Rapids) and Wakeman Trust (London).

them out using any version they like. We guarantee that after reviewing this group of texts with an open mind, the reader will never again accept the wild and glib assertions about the baptism of the Spirit which are retailed in the books of charismatic (and 'higher-life' or 'deeper-life') authors.

Before reviewing the texts, allow me to say a word about the importance of this issue. The idea that there is a baptism of the Spirit after conversion has sent many Christians soaring into a cloud-cuckoo-land of unreal emotional experiences, imagined revelations, and even delusions of perfect holiness. Countless others have been plunged into heartache and confusion because they could not get the 'baptism' they sought.

Yet every day, in charismatic gatherings large and small, people are being goaded into seeking this blessing. In a fevered environment, urged on by the prayers and appeals of others, they receive the laying-on of hands, and are taught how to begin to utter sounds that will 'trigger' their speaking in a tongue.

Some become so desperate to obtain the 'baptism' that their priorities change entirely. Instead of wanting simply to please and serve the Lord by their witness and increasing holiness, their supreme objective becomes that of getting a dramatic sensation of the Spirit in their life. They hear and read the incessant boasts of the 'Spirit-filled' people, and all that they claim to do, and become convinced that authentic

Christianity is a matter of ecstatic feelings, and even of receiving personal revelations and mysterious powers.

In today's environment of spiritual confusion, it is essential that we realise that the only baptism of the Spirit mentioned in the Bible is the gracious act of the Spirit when He comes to dwell within the believer at the time of conversion. Once He is within the soul, we have Him and we possess Him entirely. Of course, we shall want an increasing experience of His strengthening and illumination, but we must never look for an extra, additional baptism. We must not crave ecstatic, curious, mystical experiences, as though a large 'part' of the Spirit has been omitted from His entry into our lives at conversion.

Our task, once we are converted, is to begin immediately to co-operate with the Spirit, to walk by His power, and to prove His helpfulness more and more. It is as we walk in the Spirit that we will taste and know more of His power and blessing.

In the light of the claims which are being made in support of a further baptism with the Spirit *after* conversion, can it be proved that conversion includes the entire entry of the Spirit into the life of the believer? Is this a matter which is open to debate because the Scriptures are unclear? The fact is that the Bible is unmistakably clear on this subject. We are provided with a large array of texts which prove utterly and repeatedly that the Holy Spirit comes personally to dwell within every child of God *at conversion*, and not in stages.

Here are the 'proof texts' which establish the traditional reformed teaching beyond all doubt. In this chapter they are presented for convenience in order of their appearance in the Bible.

(1) Acts 2

The first is in *Acts 2.38*, where Peter says – 'Repent, and be baptised every one of you in the name of Jesus Christ for the remission of sins, and ye shall receive the gift of the Holy Ghost.'

In this text it is made clear that the experience of repenting and coming to Christ is totally bound up with the giving of the gift of the Holy Spirit. The unqualified promise of God is that the Holy Spirit will definitely come to people when they are converted.

This would seem to be an unanswerable proof text, but those who want to separate between the Holy Spirit's work at conversion, and a subsequent baptism, say that Peter is not referring to *baptism* with the Holy Spirit, but merely to an *initial gift* of the Spirit. They agree that the Holy Spirit is involved at conversion, but they say that this is something which the Spirit does by Himself, whereas Christ promised that He would personally baptise His people with the Holy Ghost.

By making this unusual distinction, they ingeniously

produce two baptisms out of one. So, according to these teachers, there remains another blessing to be experienced after conversion. (Dr Martyn Lloyd-Jones, though not strictly a charismatic, taught this idea in the last years of his ministry.)

However, Peter disqualifies this rather hair-splitting approach by telling us that the gift of the Spirit which he speaks about is the very same baptism of the Spirit which the Lord Jesus promised to give. He says – 'This Jesus hath God raised up, whereof we all are witnesses. Therefore being by the right hand of God exalted, and having received of the Father the promise of the Holy Ghost, he hath shed forth this, which ye now see and hear' *(Acts 2.32-33)*.

In other words, the gift of the Spirit poured out on the Day of Pentecost (and promised subsequently to every believer at conversion) was nothing other than the gift of the Holy Spirit as promised by Christ. There can therefore be no further baptism after this.

Peter says that this baptism will come to 'every one' who repents, and this will continue to happen throughout the ongoing history of the Church, 'For the promise is unto you, and to your children, and to all that are afar off, even as many as the Lord our God shall call' *(Acts 2.39)*. Wherever the Gospel is preached, among all nations, and for all subsequent generations, the gift of the Holy Spirit will come to sinners at the time they repent and are saved.

What was the result of the Holy Spirit's coming to those who were converted on the Day of Pentecost? Did they speak in tongues? Did they work healing miracles? As far as the vast majority of converts were concerned, the answer is – no. When people become influenced by charismatic teaching they immediately assume that the gifts of tongues, prophecy and healing were distributed among all the 3,000 converts on the Day of Pentecost. But although there is a very detailed description of the new lifestyle and pattern of behaviour of these converts, there is not one reference to ordinary believers manifesting such gifts.

The impression which commonly prevails among charismatic believers is simply not in line with the data in the New Testament. At the most, only the 120 original disciples are said to have spoken in foreign languages which they had never learned. There is no mention of the 3,000 doing so, nor the vast number who were converted soon afterwards. And Luke says that only the members of the apostolic band worked healing miracles.

The converts at the time of Pentecost received the Spirit personally and individually as they were converted, and the result was that they – 'continued stedfastly in the apostles' doctrine', and so on. They became devoted to the Word of God, gained a deep spiritual bond with other converts, discovered how to really pray and worship, and were filled with awe and wonder – all because spiritual things had become so real to them. These effects are all listed in *Acts 2.42-47*, along with a description of their unity of heart, their sacrificial sharing of goods, and their great fervour and sincerity of heart. *These* were the results of the Spirit entering their lives at conversion – not speaking in tongues or the working of miracles.

Of course, there was also a public dimension to the outpouring of the Spirit upon the new Christian Church on the Day of Pentecost. At the inauguration day of the Church, the Spirit came upon certain chosen disciples enabling them to speak in foreign languages, declaring the wonderful works of God. However, in the case of the vast crowd of new converts, the baptism of the Spirit did not result in outward signs and wonders, but in personal transformation, as their hearts were changed to love and serve the Lord. Thus the outpouring of the Spirit had a public dimension, to mark the founding of the Church, but chiefly it had a *personal, individual* dimension in the heart of each convert, and it is this aspect of the Spirit's baptism which continues until the end of time.

(2) Romans 5

Our second text to prove that the baptism of the Spirit takes place only at conversion is *Romans 5.1-5.* In this vital passage Paul writes – 'Therefore being justified by faith, we have peace with God through our

Lord Jesus Christ: by whom also we have access by faith into this grace wherein we stand, and rejoice in hope of the glory of God. And . . . the love of God is shed abroad in our hearts by the Holy Ghost which is given unto us.'

When is the Holy Ghost given to us? Paul answers – at the time of our justification, or at conversion. The wonderful experience of having the love of God shed abroad in our hearts is rooted back in our conversion. Newer translations usually make the passage even clearer by bringing out the *tense* of Paul's statement in the original Greek: 'The love of God has been poured out within our hearts through the Holy Spirit *who was given* to us.'

Some teachers drive a great wedge between the experience of conversion described in *Romans 5.1*, and the deep experience of love described in *Romans 5.5*, saying that the love of God is shed abroad in our hearts when we get a subsequent baptism of the Spirit. But the whole point of Paul's statement is to say that the receiving of the Spirit is the comfort and privilege of *everyone* who has been born again.

(3) Romans 8

Romans 8.9 and *8.15* are also verses which prove that the baptism of the Spirit occurs at conversion. In verse 9 Paul says: 'But ye are not in the flesh, but in the Spirit, if so be that the Spirit of God dwell in you. Now if any man have not the Spirit of Christ, he is none of his.' In verse 15 he says – 'For ye have not received the spirit of bondage again to fear; but ye have received the Spirit of adoption, whereby we cry, Abba, Father.'

We note that Paul gives the Holy Spirit a name – *the Spirit of adoption.* Conversion involves our being adopted into the family of God. It is the Holy Spirit Who brings this about and Who teaches us to say, 'Abba, Father,' the intimate, familiar cry of every child of God.

Nothing could be more artificial and forced than to split this passage into two parts, claiming that the second part suddenly begins to speak of a special and rarefied experience received through a second blessing of the Spirit. The plain and natural sense of the passage is:

(a) Every Christian, however young in the faith, has the Holy Spirit dwelling within. (In other words, the Spirit enters at conversion.)

(b) The 'Abba, Father' instinct enters our hearts with the indwelling Spirit from the very moment of *adoption* or conversion, and not at some later stage.

(4) 1 Corinthians 6

1 Corinthians 6 includes verses which prove that the gift of the Spirit is part of our conversion. Paul says (v 11) – 'Ye are washed . . . sanctified . . . justified in the name of the Lord Jesus, and by the Spirit of our

God.' Then he says (vv 19-20) – 'Know ye not that your body is the temple of the Holy Ghost which is in you, which ye have of God, and ye are not your own? For ye are bought with a price.'

In these verses Paul addresses *all* believers and challenges them to live sanctified lives on the grounds that as saved people they are automatically indwelt by the Holy Spirit. He indwells from the time we are 'bought with a price', which means from the day of our conversion.

(5) 1 Corinthians 12

1 Corinthians 12.13 is particularly important for this study because it is the only occasion in Paul's epistles where the term *baptism* is used in connection with the Holy Spirit.* This verse shows very clearly that the baptism of the Spirit occurs at conversion. Paul says – 'For by one Spirit are we all baptised into one body, whether we be Jews or gentiles, whether we be bond or free; and have been all made to drink into one Spirit.'

Every believer has been baptised into (which means

---

*Baptism by the Spirit is mentioned only seven times in the entire New Testament. Four of these references are in the Gospels, and all record John the Baptist saying that Christ would baptise with the Spirit. One text is the promise of Christ to baptise with the Spirit *(Acts 1.5)*. Another text is *Acts 11.16*, which is about the 'mini-Pentecost' in the house of Cornelius.

placed into) the body of Christ by the Holy Spirit. Obviously, it is at conversion that we enter the family or body of Christ. As a result, all have been made to drink of the same Holy Spirit, which means that the Holy Spirit is within each one.

Some teachers engage in the same ingenious hair-splitting over this verse as over the words of Peter on the Day of Pentecost. They insist that because this is a baptism carried out by the Spirit Himself, it cannot be the same as the baptism *with* the Spirit which Christ promised to give to believers. However, being 'made to drink into one Spirit' is without doubt the same thing as being baptised with the Spirit by Christ.

We may be certain of this because Paul uses here the very word for the baptism of the Spirit which the Lord Jesus Himself used in *John 7.37-39*. Note how the Lord used the word *drink* as a description of the receiving of the Spirit:–

> 'In the last day, that great day of the feast, Jesus stood and cried, saying, If any man thirst, let him come unto me, and drink. He that believeth on me, as the scripture hath said, out of his belly shall flow rivers of living water. (But this spake he of the Spirit, which they that believe on him should receive: for the Holy Ghost was not yet given; because that Jesus was not yet glorified.)'

When we come to Christ for salvation and drink of Him, we automatically drink of the Holy Spirit as well, and He dwells within us from that moment. *1 Corinthians 12.13*, therefore, proves that *all* believers, at conversion, are placed into the body of Christ by the Spirit, and simultaneously baptised with the Holy Spirit.

In view of the fact that Paul refers to Spirit-baptism only once in all his epistles, and then strictly in connection with conversion, how can people hijack the term to describe a second, subsequent experience of the Spirit? Let us be clear on this point – the inspired apostle had never heard of this teaching!

(6) Galatians 3

Galatians 3.2 proves beyond all argument that the Holy Spirit is poured out by Christ at the time that sinners come to saving faith. The Galatians were being drawn away into the error of justification by works. In this context Paul exclaims – 'This only would I learn of you, Received ye the Spirit by the works of the law, or by the hearing of faith?' *(Galatians 3.2.)* Clearly, he is saying that the Holy Spirit is imparted to believers when they hear the Truth and believe.

A few verses later *(Galatians 3.13-14)* Paul reminds his readers that the promise of the Holy Spirit is received through faith in the redeeming work of Christ. Once again, therefore, the receiving of Christ's promise of the Spirit is linked with the moment of *saving* faith.

(7) Galatians 4

In *Galatians 4.4-6* the link between conversion and the receiving of the Holy Spirit is emphasised yet again as Paul says – 'But when the fulness of the time was come, God sent forth his Son, made of a woman, made under the law, to redeem them that were under the law, that we might receive the adoption of sons. And because ye are sons, God hath sent forth the Spirit of his Son into your hearts, crying, Abba, Father.'

Surely the fact could not be more clearly expressed! At the time that we receive adoption as children, God sends the Spirit into our hearts, enabling us to cry, 'Abba, Father!' 'Therefore,' Paul goes on to say in the very next verse, 'you are no longer a slave, but a son.' This is nothing other than the baptism of the Spirit by God, and it is given to us along with sonship or daughterhood of God. Therefore every true believer without exception receives this blessing at the time of conversion. In texts like this there is no basis whatsoever for the idea that the baptism of the Spirit is a *subsequent* blessing enjoyed only by some believers.

(8) Ephesians 1.3

In *Ephesians 1.3* neither the baptism nor the indwelling of the Holy Spirit are mentioned, but the verse nevertheless totally eliminates the idea that Christian believers may be divided into 'haves' and 'have-nots' on the matter of whether they have been baptised with the Spirit. *All* the 'saints' at Ephesus are said by Paul to have been blessed 'with all spiritual blessings in heavenly places in Christ'.

Paul insists here that every believer is given *every* spiritual blessing by virtue of being in Christ. As Dr William Hendriksen says, 'The very word *every* clearly proves that it would be wrong to subtract even a single invisible bounty from the list of those vast benefits divine which we in Christ possess, yet the context indicates that the apostle is thinking particularly of those that are mentioned in the present paragraph, namely election . . . redemption . . . and certification (sealing) as sons and heirs.'

God says that *every* spiritual blessing, including the seal of the Spirit, comes to every person the moment he is 'in Christ'. We must resist any interpretation which siphons off either the sealing or baptism of the Spirit and makes it the possession of only *some*, privileged believers. The idea is completely out of line with all the grand apostolic statements.

(9) Ephesians 1.13-14

Ephesians 1.13-14 provides yet another solid proof text for the doctrine that the baptism of the Holy Spirit *always* occurs at conversion. These verses read: 'In whom ye also trusted, after that ye heard the word of truth, the gospel of your salvation: in whom also after that ye believed, ye were sealed with that holy Spirit of promise, which is the earnest of our inheritance until the redemption of the purchased possession, unto the praise of his glory.'

'After you heard,' says Paul, 'and having believed' (this is the literal sense of the Greek), 'you were sealed.' Being sealed with the Holy Spirit is the inevitable consequence of believing. It is part of conversion.

The sealing of the Spirit refers to the receiving of authenticating signs, by which the new convert (and those who look on) may be certain that the Spirit has given him new life, and placed him on the road to Heaven. The idea of sealing also includes security.

This sealing is clearly an aspect of the baptism and indwelling of the Spirit, for the believer is sealed *with* (not *by*) the Spirit. The form of words indicates that the promised Holy Spirit is given, and this has the effect of *sealing* the believer.

This occurs as a pledge or 'deposit' to assure us that our salvation will be carried through to Heaven by the Lord. The plain meaning of the passage is that God gives this wonderful guarantee to *every* recipient of grace. He does not merely give it to some, or even to many, but to all. Those teachers who say that this is the experience of only *some* believers, make total nonsense of the illustration which is given.

Everyone understands the value of a guarantee. What trader gives a guarantee to some customers while withholding it from others? If people buy new houses or new appliances, they expect the guarantee to be certain. They would be unable to believe their ears if the salesman said, 'A guarantee? Oh, you may get one; on the other hand you may not. You will have to see as time goes on whether you are one of the fortunate ones who is given a guarantee.'

When God gives a pledge and a guarantee to His people, He gives it to them all. Accordingly, when we believe, the Holy Spirit enters in, and His first gracious work is to give us a foretaste of our future blessings; a 'placental' experience of spiritual benefits.

(10) Ephesians 4

Ephesians 4.30 also affirms that all believers are sealed by the Holy Spirit, and not merely some. Modern translations correctly employ the past tense in this verse: 'And do not grieve the Holy Spirit of God, by whom you *were* sealed for the day of redemption' *(NASB)*. Paul does not say that some of them were sealed, nor even most of them, but he presumes that all of them were sealed when they were brought into the Christian life.

(11) 1 Thessalonians 1

1 Thessalonians 1.5-6 firmly places the Spirit's baptism of joy right alongside the experience of conversion. Here Paul says – 'For our gospel came not unto you in word only, but also in power, and in the Holy Ghost, and in much assurance; as ye know what manner of men we were among you for your sake. And ye became followers of us, and of the Lord, having received the word in much affliction, with joy of the Holy Ghost.'

The people savingly grasped and received the Word, receiving as they did so the joy of the Holy Spirit. Joy is a fruit of the Spirit *(Galatians 5.22)*, and therefore the giving of joy by the Spirit presupposes the entry and baptism of the Spirit.

(12) 1 John 4

1 John 4.12-13 is one of two similar proof texts in the same epistle. It reads: 'If we love one another, God dwelleth in us, and his love is perfected in us. Hereby know we that we dwell in him, and he in us, because he hath given us of his Spirit.' Also, at the end of the previous chapter, John says – 'And hereby we know that he abideth in us, by the Spirit which he hath given us.'

In these words the apostle John makes no allowance for the possibility that some truly converted Christians may not have received the baptism of (or with) the Spirit. In John's 'tests of life', the baptism and indwelling of the Holy Spirit are inseparable from the presence of spiritual life itself.

The traditional view

The natural sense of all these passages is that the baptism of the Holy Spirit (and His sealing) occurs as part of the conversion of the believer. By contrast, passages which are claimed in support of a separate, post-conversion baptism of the Spirit are never plain and straightforward. Complex exegetical gymnastics have to be accomplished in order to make any semblance of a case for this second blessing.

The texts we have just examined confirm the historic position of mainstream evangelicalism on the baptism of the Spirit. This is the viewpoint so perfectly summarised in the *Baptist Confession of Faith of 1689* in the following words: 'All those that are justified . . . receive the Spirit of adoption . . . are enabled to cry "Abba, Father," are pitied, protected, provided for, and chastened by Him, as by a Father; yet never cast off; but sealed to the day of redemption . . . ' (chapter 12).

What about the Ephesus twelve?

When charismatic and second-blessing writers present their case for a baptism of the Spirit in addition to conversion, they nearly always point to what happened at Ephesus when Paul discovered a group of believers there. The reasoning goes along these lines: Paul found a company of about twelve men in the synagogue who believed that Christ was the Messiah.

On discovering that they were ignorant of the Holy Spirit, he laid hands upon them and they received the Spirit and spoke in tongues. All this proves that the baptism of the Spirit is to be received as a separate blessing, after conversion, and that it may (most charismatics say *will*) be accompanied by speaking in tongues.

Is this a sound and reasonable interpretation of the events at Ephesus? The resounding answer of the vast majority of evangelical Bible commentators through church history is that it is not. The traditional evangelical explanation of what took place at Ephesus is set out in an appendix at the end of this book, together with the reasons why it is wrong to read into the passage a second baptism of the Spirit. Readers are invited to study this appendix – *The Case of the Ephesus Twelve.*

2. *Is a Second Baptism Needed for Assurance?*

MOST OF THOSE WHO teach the need for a baptism of the Spirit after conversion, claim that this is essential for sanctification. This is the prevailing viewpoint among the majority of charismatics, and all 'higher-life' teachers. They say that once a Christian receives this extra baptism, all the effort of living a holy life is taken over by the indwelling Holy Spirit, leaving no battle for the believer.

Some teachers, however, especially in recent years, have advanced a different benefit as the chief value of this additional baptism of the Holy Spirit. Their idea is that such a baptism is the only source of truly satisfying joy and assurance. The need of a second baptism for assurance is argued from the words of Paul in

Romans 8.15: 'For ye have not received the spirit of bondage again to fear; but ye have received the Spirit of adoption, whereby we cry, Abba, Father.'

Those who see a special baptism as essential for full assurance attach tremendous significance to the words – 'Abba, Father.' They seize this expression and turn it into an exalted cry of ecstatic certainty and assurance. They say, 'This is nothing other than a most intimate form of assurance. Here, a glorious sense of sonship wells up within the believer and almost overwhelms his soul. At such a moment the believer can have no doubt whatsoever that he is a child of God, for he is filled with sublime joy. This is a direct infusion of great assurance which is clearly not the general experience of most Christians today. It is nothing less than a baptism with the Holy Spirit!'

The first comment to be made on this interpretation is that the context warns against it. We must remember that Paul has just said (in verse 9) that the Spirit of God already dwells in every true Christian, without exception. We must also note (as seen in chapter 1 of this book) that Paul says that the 'Spirit of adoption' causes us to say, 'Abba, Father!' which connects this cry with the time of our adoption (or conversion).

Furthermore, it should be noted that the advocates of a special baptism greatly exaggerate the meaning of the words 'Abba, Father!' There is no justification for inflating them to speak of a rarefied and heavenly sensation of assurance. Some writers get completely carried away at this point. They have a wildly romantic and fanciful idea of the meaning of the term.

Paul's words are meant to be of great comfort to ordinary Christians. They were never intended to teach the availability of an *extraordinary* level of assurance resulting from a special baptism, and they should not be snatched away from ordinary believers in order to nourish the quest for ecstatic experiences.

Romans 8.15-16 is meant to be a very reassuring passage for all believers. Paul tells us that one of the benefits of true conversion is that while we may go through periods of failure and trial, we always have admission into the presence of our Father, for we know how to pray. We know the way 'home'. We can always find our way to the throne of grace, assured that we are accepted in Christ, and there we may pour out our hearts before the Lord.

The passage in no way requires remarkable sensations of joy and glory. It simply says that because we are adopted children we instinctively know how to cry out to our Father, and we may have intimate access into His presence at any time.

If we are truly converted, we do not have the superstitious, frightened attitude of pagans, who desperately offer sacrifices in a vain hope that their gods will hear them. Nor do we, like the formal worshippers among the Jews, hope against hope that priests, sacrifices and other ceremonies will secure the favour of an unknowable God. Whether we are deeply or moderately assured in our feelings, we are certain that God will forgive us and receive us because He is *our Father*, and we are adopted children. Therefore we do not shrink from coming before Him in prayer. This is what Paul is saying, and it gives comfort and encouragement to us all, and not only to 'super-spiritual' people!

A small child may be resentful towards his parents because of some punishment he has received, or because he wants something which has been withheld from him. Or he may be completely preoccupied in play, so that he is not, for the time being, interested in his parents. But does he ever lose his awareness that he is his parents' child? Does he forget that he belongs in the house? Does he become afraid to run to his parents if he needs something? Does he forget the way from the garden into the house? Or does he forget what his parents look like?

Paul's great cry of 'Abba, Father' simply means that we know that God is our own Father, and that we can always count on His care. 'Abba' was the personal and familiar Aramaic word for father, and it is used by Paul to emphasise the personal bond between believers and their heavenly Father. It was a word which was used regardless of how one felt. Sad and troubled people would use this simple and beautiful word in addressing their father, just as elated, happy people would. The Lord Jesus Christ used it in the Garden of Gethsemane when His soul was 'exceeding sorrowful unto death'. He prayed that the hour might pass from Him. 'Sore amazed, and . . . very heavy', He prayed, 'Abba, Father!'

If the Lord Jesus could use this term in His greatest hour of anguish, can it be true that it exclusively signifies elevated, ecstatic, joyous feelings?

Even the word *cry* is pressed into service by Spirit-baptism teachers in support of the idea that this term suggests a wonderful level of feeling flowing from a special baptism of the Spirit. It is claimed that the great intensity of the Greek verb confirms the depth of assurance being experienced by the one who cries, 'Abba, Father.'

However, the very same verb is used in the Bible in connection with cries of anguish, dismay, need, and even hatred and opposition. It is used of the final cry of the Saviour *(Matthew 27.50)* in the hour of His forsakenness, when He yielded up the spirit.

It is certainly a very feelingful cry, but it can be the cry of a very down-hearted, needy, despondent soul, just as much as that of a rejoicing and assured person.

Without doubt, the plain sense of this 'Abba, Father' passage is to teach that all genuine children know how to approach their heavenly Father, and can fall before Him in true repentance and with heartfelt love at any time. To find in this term evidence for a higher, mystical experience involves fanciful and novel exegesis of the passage.

However, while it is wrong to read into 'Abba, Father' a sublime experience of assurance resulting from a second blessing, there is a wonderful form of assurance which comes to us from the ordinary work of the Spirit in our lives, and this we shall examine in the next chapter.

3. How Does the Spirit Witness With Our Spirit?

PAUL HAS BEEN SPEAKING in *Romans 8.15* of how the Holy Spirit imparts to believers a personal consciousness that God is now their Father. Then, in verse 16, he turns to the way in which the Spirit bears witness to their salvation in a more direct way. He says: 'The Spirit itself beareth witness with our spirit, that we are the children of God.' The question is, how does the Holy Spirit witness with our spirit?

First, we must be clear on what Paul does not mean here. He does not say that the Holy Spirit is poured out in a special baptism, thereby flooding the soul with *direct* divine assurance. While our sovereign, gracious God may at times grant very remarkable seasons of special assurance to His people, this is not what is in mind in this verse, for Paul is presenting the normal, everyday experience of Christians.

Some writers describe only two forms of assurance: first, that which is deduced from the Bible, and second, an elevated form which comes directly from the Spirit of God. They regard the first as a rather inferior form of assurance, because believers must glean it for themselves. They must read the Bible and find passages which describe the signs or tests of true conversion (eg: *Acts 2.42 ff; 1 John*). Then, as they read, they will be able to say, 'This has certainly happened to me, therefore I must be truly saved.'

But then, we are told, we must move on to the higher, superior type of assurance – the overwhelming sense of wonder and sonship which comes directly from the Spirit as the result of a special baptism. In reality, the gift of direct and intense assurance is rather occasional. It would appear to be a special kindness, given chiefly to believers in times of great oppression or grief or exertion. It cannot be worked up, for it is a sovereign prerogative of the Spirit.

It is wrong to teach that *this* is the normal experience of the believer, because to do so gives great alarm to all who see that this is not their everyday experience, and throws many earnest souls into seeking a special Spirit-baptism.

A surprising feature of this teaching is that it leaps right over the most common form of assurance of all.

Indeed, it simply does not recognise its existence. The fact is, that lying between the assurance which may be deduced from the Bible, and the very wonderful kind which the Spirit gives in a direct way, there is a rich and rewarding form of regular, daily assurance available to all believers, and this is the form referred to by Paul in *Romans 8.16.* It is the constant interaction of the Holy Spirit in our lives as we pray to God for help in dealing with our sins, and also for His help with the many other needs and problems which we face every day, especially in our witness and service for the Lord.

We derive immense and constant assurance from the obvious help we receive from the Spirit in the continuous flow of answers to our prayers. Included in our prayers are many for guidance and help in understanding the Word, and all are abundantly answered.

It is so sad that some teachers, in their preoccupation with the idea of a special baptism, entirely overlook the everyday supply of assurance which springs from experimental Christian living, or day-to-day praying.

It is clear from all that Paul has been saying in the preceding verses that this is in his mind when he speaks of the Spirit witnessing with our spirit. He has just said: 'Therefore, brethren, we are debtors, not to the flesh, to live after the flesh. For if ye live after the flesh, ye shall die: but if ye through the Spirit do mortify the deeds of the body, ye shall live. For as many as are led by the Spirit of God, they are the sons of God' *(Romans 8.12-14).*

The subject here is putting to death the deeds of the flesh by the help of the Spirit. Those who prayerfully engage in the fight against personal sin find to their joy that they are actively helped by the Spirit, and this is a grand source of encouragement, as we shall see in chapter six – *Are We to Fight Sin?*

Paul gives us a picture of Christians whose consciences are (as the result of prayer) made lively by the Spirit, and who therefore become concerned about sin. They long to make progress, and they practise self-examination, and pray for help to put to death wrong thoughts, desires and actions. Thus walking in daily co-operation with the Spirit, they experience *through the help they receive* the sure 'witness' of the Spirit that they are children of God.

This form of assurance is truly authenticating, because only genuinely regenerate people hunger and thirst after righteousness, hate their sin, and long to please and serve the Lord in obedience to His commandments.

But supremely, the Holy Spirit confirms that He is our Guardian by His unmistakable help in answer to prayer. Time after time we are given grace to overcome some trial, and strengthened to stand up to great difficulties. Repeatedly we are given cause to thank and praise God for hearing and answering our prayers, and so the Spirit adds His testimony to ours, that we are the children of God.

If, therefore, we lack assurance, it may be that our flow of 'evidence' (through answered prayer) has dried up. Have we stopped praying? Do we no longer seek specific help about particular problems or sins? Have we stopped noticing the answers to our prayers?

Why do we crave after *direct* assurance, as though we had no evidence from answered prayer? Are we not engaged in any hard Christian service, which leads us to earnest prayer, and therefore to the very many answers which will inevitably follow?

Let us leave the provision of *direct* feelings of assurance to the Lord. If our God chooses to pour upon us at some time a special awareness that we are His children, and a special sense of His love for us, then that is His sovereign prerogative. It is not the everyday experience of the believer. If it were, then this would not be a life of faith! Let us not demand the special benefits as if they were our daily right.

Let us rejoice in the fact that our faith may be wonderfully strengthened as we read the signs of conversion in the Word. But let it be strengthened even more as we notice and give thanks for the vast number of clear answers to our prayers.

The *help* of the Spirit is one of the great themes of *Romans 8*. If we do not strive for personal advance in sanctification, or if we have no avenue of Christian service, and bear no burdens in the Lord's work, then we will have no burning needs, and few truly significant things to pray for. Consequently we will suffer a terrible lack of evidence of the Spirit's help, and therefore have little assurance. Those who are 'hearers only' miss most of the real blessing.

It is believers who lack assurance for these reasons who begin to crave a more direct form of assurance. Be warned: this is the high road to mysticism and self-delusion. Some believers want a blessing, but not on the Lord's terms. They want assurance without Christian service or commitment. But the Lord has determined that most assurance will come through the evidences of the Spirit's help in daily sanctification, witness and service.

So vitally important is this matter that it must be proved by reference to other passages of Scripture. Where else, then, does Scripture spell out the fact that much of our assurance must come from experiencing the interaction and help of the Spirit in answer to our prayers, especially prayers for help in sanctification and service?

The following paragraphs provide a rapid review of key passages which show that throughout the New Testament the apostolic teaching never varies on this point. Assurance is constantly described as flowing from the struggle against sin, and from the practice of praying to God for help in all the affairs of life.

Believers are meant to build up a great memory-bank of all God's goodness and power towards them, and thus become increasingly *convinced.*

Look, for example, at the prayer of Paul for the Christians at Ephesus, which begins in *Ephesians 1.17*, proceeds into a glorious doctrinal digression, and resumes as a prayer from *Ephesians 3.14.*

Paul first prays that the Holy Spirit will illuminate the Ephesian believers (already sealed with the Spirit at their conversion according to *Ephesians 1.13*) so that they may fully grasp the wonder of their future inheritance, and the power of God in saving, keeping, protecting and sanctifying them on the way to glory. Two great sources of assurance are referred to in the opening part of the prayer – the Word, and the power of God.

Then, in *Ephesians 3.14-16*, Paul prays: 'For this cause I bow my knees unto the Father of our Lord Jesus Christ, of whom the whole family in heaven and earth is named, that he would grant you, according to the riches of his glory, to be strengthened with might by his Spirit in the inner man.'

Note once again that these Ephesians were already *sealed* with the Spirit at conversion, yet they still needed to be 'strengthened with might by his Spirit in the inner man'.

Even though the Spirit is within us we constantly need strengthening because the Holy Spirit does not give us all the strength we require from the first day of conversion. The strengthening of the Spirit is something continuous, and even conditional, for we must pray for help, and keep the terms and conditions for blessing.

What will we need all this strengthening for? Why will we need *might*? (The Greek means 'being made able' or 'given capability'.) The language of Paul reminds us that while here we are in a battle in the service for the Lord. To succeed and to prevail we shall need constant power and strength.

Paul is not praying for lazy Christians who want assurance without attempting to serve the Lord or struggle against their sin. He is praying for believers who will practise self-denial and commit themselves to the battle of spreading the Gospel, speaking for the Saviour, and serving shoulder to shoulder with fellow-labourers in the church. He is praying for those who will practise regular self-examination and fight against the allurements of this world and personal sin.

It is these believers for whom Paul also prays 'that Christ may dwell in your hearts by faith; that ye, being rooted and grounded in love, may be able to comprehend . . . the breadth, and length, and depth, and height; and to know the love of Christ, which passeth knowledge . . .' Take first the words – '*rooted and grounded* in love'. As we pray for help in holiness and service, we receive strength to be stable, patient and disciplined, and we then derive much assurance from the fact that the Spirit enables such weak, unstable people as we are to stand firm. We find we are not uprooted and hurled aside like ill-rooted trees in a storm, but that we stand firm against all the temptations of the devil, the temptations of the world, and the inclination to laziness or cowardice in witness.

Paul's prayer 'that Christ may dwell in your hearts' also belongs to the battle context. This confirms that Christ means most to us, and comes closest to us, when we are in the thick of the battle.

Paul prays that believers may grasp 'the breadth, and length, and depth, and height' and know 'the love of Christ, which passeth knowledge'. We desire the assurance which shines out from these words, but let us never forget that the route to this assurance passes first through the battlefield where sin is fought, and also through the servants' hall!

The 'formula' for assurance and blessedness is the same throughout the New Testament. How do we obtain assurance? First things first: we must want to please the Lord, to deal with our sin, and to serve Him zealously. Then we shall find ourselves with much need of help, and we shall pray many prayers. Much of our praying will be for our avenue of Christian service – our Sunday School class perhaps, and the effectiveness of our teaching. The result will be an experience of constant strengthening and answered prayer, and that experience will in turn assure our hearts, greatly uplifting us, and drawing us close to Christ.

Paul prays 'that Christ may dwell in your hearts *by faith*'. What does the word *faith* mean? It means – to be convinced, to be fully persuaded. This is very largely a result of what has gone before. If we are praying often and receiving answers to our prayers we shall build up considerable evidence of the goodness and power of God as He interacts with our lives, and we shall be increasingly convinced, persuaded and certain that His promises are true, His Word is right, and that Christ Jesus is our glorious Lord and Saviour. Soon it will become much harder for the devil or anyone else to persuade us that there is no God, no Christ, or that we are not truly converted.

This deepened conviction and certainty will, of course, bring Christ closer to us. Paul's prayer, therefore, does not refer to rarefied, ecstatic sensations of assurance imparted to us by God in a direct way (though such experiences may truly be given at times by the Lord). Paul's words speak of an assurance which is ours through experiencing the constant goodness, power, comfort and consolation of the Lord in answer to our prayers.

For confirmation of this we note the opening words of Paul's doxology – 'Now unto him that is able to do exceeding abundantly above all that we ask or think, according to *the power that worketh in us . . .*' *(Ephesians 3.20)*. The glorious knowledge of Christ in a personal and assured form is essentially connected with the experience of practical blessing.

Of course, this is not the whole story. Our study of the Word and our heartfelt worship also draw us close to Christ and give us assurance. We are assured as our minds are illuminated to grasp the deep things of the Word.

Nevertheless, we must appreciate that much assurance flows from active involvement in the basic spiritual duties that we have reviewed, namely the sacrificial yielding of our time and energies in holiness and the service of the Lord.

Some believers today seem to be saying, 'Oh, I do not want that. I do not want the duty of fighting against my sin. I do not want to renounce my wonderful career ambitions and be involved in Christian service. I want a direct blessing.' But Christ can never be entirely at home in such hearts.

The idea that believers can count on a direct form of assurance, unconnected with proving the Lord in the ways we have described, is so prevalent today that one has to prove the old doctrine many times over before the point is thoroughly received.

Hebrews 6.11-12 emphasises this truth yet again. Here the Spirit of God states that assurance is obtained only by diligent application to spiritual duties. 'And we desire that every one of you do shew the same diligence to the full assurance of hope unto the end: that ye be not slothful, but followers of them who through faith and patience inherit the promises.'

Immediately before these verses the writer had referred to the Hebrews' 'work and labour of love'. They were zealous, earnest, striving, active believers, who proved the help of the Lord in their lives. The *NASB* renders the crucial statement very significantly: 'And we desire that each one of you show the same diligence so as to realize the full assurance of hope until the end.'

The apostle Peter adds his voice to the chorus of testimony that this is the chief pathway to assurance. In *2 Peter 1.5-8* there is a remarkable sequence of exhortations telling us to give all diligence to add to our faith virtue, and so on. Knowledge, self-control, patience, godliness, brotherly kindness and love all come into the list of things to which diligence must be applied. Then Peter gives a warning and a promise:

> 'But he that lacketh these things is blind, and cannot see afar off, and hath forgotten that he was purged from his old sins. Wherefore the rather, brethren, give diligence to make your calling and election sure: for if ye do these things, ye shall never fall: for so an entrance shall be ministered unto you abundantly into the everlasting kingdom of our Lord and Saviour Jesus Christ' *(2 Peter 1.9-11).*

If we are not engaged in prayer for help and progress in the development of godly character and virtues then we will lose our spiritual 'sight' (though not, of course, our salvation). We shall feel lost and in darkness. We will even forget what it felt like when we were first pardoned and our hearts were lifted up in new-born happiness.

On the other hand, if we have a constant experience of answered prayer in the pursuit of practical holiness and service, then we shall never *fall* (which means 'stumble') into barrenness (v 8), fruitlessness or despondency. On the contrary, we shall *feel* like people who are entering into the kingdom!

If anyone has the slightest doubt that to co-operate with the Spirit in the quest for holiness is a major route to assurance, then the words of the apostle John will help. In *1 John 3.18-19* we read: 'My little children, let us not love in word, neither in tongue *[only]*; but in *deed* and in *truth.* And hereby we know that we are of the truth, and shall assure our hearts before him.'

In other words if we are concerned for holiness, and we receive the help of the Spirit as we pray to overcome our sinful traits, then this will be a great source of assurance to us.

1 John is, of course, very largely an epistle of assurance. John says – 'These things have I written unto you that believe on the name of the Son of God; that ye may know that ye have eternal life, and that ye may believe on the name of the Son of God' *(1 John 5.13).*

Yet we go through *1 John* in vain to find any mention of *direct* assurance. This is not because John, writing under inspiration, denies that God may dispense direct assurance according to His own loving will. It is because this epistle deals with the *practical* aspects of assurance. Therefore, John says with Paul: Co-operate with the Spirit of God. Pray for much help in your life. Strive to improve in righteousness, and strive to serve the Lord, and you will find that you receive such wonderful help, so many answers to your prayers, that you will gain great encouragement and certainty. Seek by this means the living interaction of the Spirit in your life.

Are we praying for help as we put to death our faults? Are we asking for strength as we resist the temptations to buy expensive things and live comfortable lives? Are we praying for help in curbing our tempers, our natural selfishness, and all other besetting sins?

What if we do not co-operate with the indwelling Spirit when He touches our consciences, and 'stands by' to respond to our cries for strength? We shall not only forfeit His help, with all the assurance which that brings, but we may well forfeit also any direct gift of assurance which the Lord may have poured out upon us. The Lord will certainly not spoil His children when they are disobedient and wayward.

We have here laboured the point about a crucial form of assurance strangely omitted from the teaching of some writers who advocate a baptism with the Spirit as the route to joy and certainty. The kind of assurance which comes from the evidence of practical daily blessing as we strive in sanctification and Christian service is probably (if we understand *1 John* correctly) the main form of assurance to believers. However, it is not the only form of assurance, and we give the following list so that no form is forgotten.

(1) Assurance may be derived from consideration of the 'marks of grace', or signs of conversion given in the Scriptures. As we see that these have been experienced by us, then we are gladdened and assured of our salvation.

(2) Assurance may be derived from a full and soul-warming view of Truth, as the Holy Spirit illuminates the mind in the reading of His Word, and as we feed upon the attributes, works and purposes of our glorious God.

(3) Evidential assurance (referred to chiefly in these pages), arising from the obvious strengthening, helping activity of the Spirit as the believer seeks prayerfully to live a sanctified life and serve the Lord, and also arising from all other glorious answers to prayer.

(4) Special assurance, in which the Holy Spirit may from time to time give an unusually deep sense of

assurance, and so bless the soul that it overflows in wonder, love and praise, and is taken up by a sense of the glory of God. Such assurance may be especially associated with times of persecution (as in the testimony of the noble army of martyrs) or grief, or special service. It is the Lord's doing, and it is very precious to the believer, but it is unscriptural to present it as the 'norm' to be sought after.

4. The Spirit of Holiness

THE GREAT HERITAGE of doctrinal teaching reflected in the books of most commentators and preachers since the Reformation says that the advance of believers in holiness is a progressive matter, involving their effort and co-operation, as well as the work of the Holy Spirit in their lives.

With the passage of time a mystical stream of teaching began to appear, which claimed that, just as we are justified by faith, so also we must be sanctified by faith. The idea was that a post-conversion baptism of the Spirit would take care of holiness, leaving us without the need for struggle and disappointment. This view was adopted by most Pentecostalists, and in more recent times by the majority of charismatics.

Before showing how the traditional route to

sanctification differs from the Spirit-baptism, 'automatic-sanctification' error, we invite readers to take a brief look at some sentences from that superb document, the *Baptist Confession of Faith of 1689* (also entitled, *Things Most Surely Believed Among Us*). This was based on the *Westminster Confession of Faith*, and expresses precisely the same teaching as other famous Confessions.

> 'They who are united to Christ, effectually called and regenerated, having a new heart and a new spirit created in them . . . are also further sanctified, really and personally . . . by His Word and Spirit dwelling in them; the dominion of the whole body of sin is destroyed . . . '

We interrupt our quotation to point out how carefully the *Confession* writers express themselves. They do not say that the whole body of sin is destroyed, but that the *dominion* of the whole body of sin is destroyed. In other words, the body of sin is still there, but it is no longer master of the life. To resume:

> '. . . the dominion of the whole body of sin is destroyed and the several lusts thereof are more and more weakened and mortified, and they *[believers]* more and more quickened and strengthened in all saving graces, to the practice of all true holiness, without which no man shall see the Lord.'

The *Confession* states very precisely that at conversion the *dominion* of sin is smashed and broken, but that the actual lusts or sinful desires are not caused to vanish. They are *progressively* weakened and put to death as believers advance in the practice of true holiness. Sanctification is described as a *progressive* work in the souls of believers.

The next paragraph in the *Confession* expands further on the existence of continuing sin (sometimes called 'residual' sin), and shows that the Spirit helps us to battle against it. Note the fighting language which is used:

> 'This sanctification is throughout, in the whole man, yet imperfect in this life; there abideth still some remnants of corruption in every part, whence ariseth a continual and irreconcilable war; the flesh lusting against the Spirit, and the Spirit against the flesh.
>
> 'In which war, although the remaining corruption for a time may much prevail, yet, through the continual supply of strength from the sanctifying Spirit of Christ, the regenerate part doth overcome; and so the saints grow in grace, perfecting holiness in the fear of God, pressing after an heavenly life, in evangelical obedience to all the commands which Christ, as Head and King, in His Word, hath prescribed to them.'

There is a fine comment on these statements in a book entitled, *The Westminster Confession Study Manual*, by G. I. Williamson:–

'The doctrine of sanctification teaches us that there

is rather a radical breach with the power and love of sin. It teaches us that established within us is a new power and love which necessitates unquenchable conflict with sin.

'The dominion of sin is broken, though the presence of sin is not entirely eliminated. Just as penicillin may break a fever, just destroying the dominion of a disease, and yet some time elapses before every trace of the disease is eliminated, so it is with sin. Just as the allied armies invaded Europe and destroyed the threat of Hitler's hope of world dominion, and yet required much more time to eradicate every vestige of it, so it is with sin.

'Sin no longer commands the heart. The main lines of communication have been destroyed. The control centre is now in the hands of God. But the alien force still carries on harassment of all kinds with all the skill, cunning and desperation of a defeated foe. As the late Professor John Murray has aptly said – there is a total difference between *surviving* sin and *reigning* sin.'

The great theologian John Owen, writing in 1652, expressed the way conversion alters the believer's relationship with sin in the following words:–

'By nature the flesh is wholly predominant constantly making the soul to sin. But when grace comes in, the habit of sin is weakened and impaired so that it shall not reign or lord it over us. But yet it is never entirely dispossessed and cast out of the soul in this life. There it will remain and work, seduce and tempt, more or less, according to its remaining strengths and advantages. Let no man think to kill sin with a few gentle strokes.'

Does all this mean that there are two natures in a Christian – the new nature which came in with conversion, and the old? To be precise, there is one predominant nature in the Christian, because the main disposition of the converted soul is to please God and to live for Him and know Him. Even in our backslidden moments we believers make ill-at-ease, unhappy worldlings. Our chief characteristic is that we love the Lord, and are 'on the Lord's side'. In this sense there is only one nature in the Christian, and this is our new nature.

But if people wish to use the term *nature* to describe any and all of our possible moods or states, then we have to agree that there are two natures, because sin is still alive in our lives. The old self is not entirely eradicated. In this sense, the old nature is still there, and must be taken account of, and fought.

There can be no victory over the old nature by the notion that we can get automatic-sanctification by the Spirit just by yielding to Him, or receiving a second baptism from Him. This theory comes under a number of names today, and there are any number of books advocating the victorious life, the higher

Christian life, Christian perfection, entire sanctification, sanctification-by-faith, full-Gospel holiness, the faith-rest-life, the release of the Spirit, and scriptural brokenness, besides the baptism of the Spirit, the fulness of the Spirit, and the second blessing.

However, the more the theory of automatic-sanctification is tried, the more it is proved to be false. Countless true believers have been persuaded that it is the biblical way, but the old nature can never be banished or suppressed without a struggle. This theory has disastrously failed countless believers by encouraging them to relax their vigilance and their battle against personal sin. Thus it has undermined godliness and caused them to fall into sin. Not only have standards of godliness fallen in the churches where these things are taught, but many people, fondly imagining that they have been sanctified by virtue of 'abiding in the Spirit' or 'abiding in Christ', have been swallowed up by pride.

Most 'traditional' evangelical pastors have had the task, at some time or other, of having to bring a touch of reality into the lives of people who imagined they were filled with the Spirit and perfectly sanctified, when in fact they lived selfish, worldly lives. Adherents of these systems of Spirit-baptism often become highly subjective and preoccupied with themselves, contrary to the unselfish, 'outward flowing' genius of true Christian character.

In addition to the failure of these ideas to produce real holiness, we must have sympathy for the casualties, and they are numerous. Many Christians have tried hard to obtain a special spiritual experience which takes away sinful behaviour only to find that nothing happens. For sincere people, the disappointment can lead to spiritual despair. They conclude that their failure to find the promised benefit is due to *their* faithless, backslidden condition, and they feel crushed and condemned.

Numerous believers have been influenced by bizarre forms of this teaching, such as the version which says that the flesh is wrapped around the spirit, suffocating it, and what we must do is humiliate and crack apart the flesh in order that the spirit may be released. This particular example of cult-like theology rose to amazing popularity in the late 1930s, and still has many advocates. It can produce intense introspection and anguish, especially in believers who possess sensitive and depressive personalities.

The doctrine of sanctification of the Bible, so well explained by the Reformers and Puritans, and then by the great majority of sound preachers until this century, insists on the believer being actively involved in the struggle against sin.

5. Attending the Wrong Classroom

IT GOES WITHOUT SAYING that the correct method of seeking holiness must be that which is taught in the Bible. But this leads to another issue – are we interpreting the Bible in a logical, sensible manner?

Unfortunately, one of the chief characteristics of Spirit-baptism teachers has been their unorthodox method of handling the Bible. They usually support their ideas by quoting verses which are wrested right out of their context and made to read differently from their plain sense.

Indeed, many who promote the second blessing claim that their viewpoint does not have to be derived logically from Scripture. They justify their novel interpretations on the grounds that they have received a special anointing of the Spirit to grasp the real but hidden meaning of the passages they quote – a meaning which other Christians fail to see because they do not have their special illumination of the Holy Spirit. Naturally, as soon as we accept this 'special anointing' notion, then we have thousands of different 'Bibles', and we lose our sure yardstick of Truth. The Word of God ceases to be a clear authority and rule for believers, because it depends upon individual 'anointing'.

We believe that the anointing of the Spirit is essential for the understanding of Scripture, but this comes with the powerful work of conversion in our souls, so that we become *spiritual* rather than *natural* people. (The apostle John, in *1 John 2.27*, indicates that this anointing is in every believer, not just 'special' people, and that it abides with them all the time.)

After conversion we continue to need the help of God, and we therefore pray for humility and discernment as we study the Scripture. But there is no special anointing after conversion which will make one Christian superior to another, and give him an entirely unique and personal view of a passage, concealed by God from other believers.

In the study of the Bible we must follow the Bible's own rules of interpretation. We consider first the plain and obvious sense of the passage. We then take care to relate the passage to its context. We compare our interpretation with other scriptures, in case we arrive at a conclusion which makes Scripture contradict itself. In controversial matters we check the meaning of words in the original language of Scripture. And we also pay respectful attention to trustworthy teachers and commentators before jumping to novel conclusions.

It has to be said that even the most noted exponents of Spirit-baptism and automatic-sanctification work in total disregard of these basic interpretive rules. If they were to respect them, their doctrines would collapse instantly.

Here is a major example of the kind of mistake they make by ignoring the basic rules of logical interpretation. These teachers constantly use texts dealing with salvation and *justification*, to teach the principles of *sanctification*!

If I am at school or college, it makes sense to attend the right lecture. It will not help me to go to the lecture room designated for chemistry if my subject is physics. If, by some absurdity, I go into the wrong class, and try to accommodate the lecture to my subject, my confusion will be nothing short of spectacular.

Yet here is the strange mistake of all sanctification-by-faith, and sanctification-by-Spirit-baptism teachers. To get their sanctification data, they have gone into the wrong classroom. The sign on the door clearly read – 'Subject: Justification'. And into that room they went to form their understanding of sanctification.

Consider how these teachers explain *Galatians 2.20.*

Paul says: 'I am crucified with Christ: nevertheless I live; yet not I, but Christ liveth in me: and the life which I now live in the flesh I live by the faith of the Son of God, who loved me, and gave himself for me.'

This verse is used to teach that in order to live holy lives we must die to ourselves. This involves our giving up all personal effort to resist sin, depending instead on Christ to manifest His power and life in us, and to entirely take over the battle. To 'die' is to give up the struggle!

However, this verse is not about our ongoing sanctification. As soon as we check on the context (the subject of the surrounding verses) we find that the whole passage is about *justification.* It is about salvation. Being *justified* is mentioned three times in the preceding verses. Paul is refuting people who taught justification by works. He is talking about how we obtain *justifying* righteousness, not sanctifying righteousness.

As it happens, *Galatians 2.20* is probably the chief anchor of automatic-sanctification teachers, and yet it has been used illegitimately. In fact, the main subject is *justification* by faith alone right through *Galatians 1, 2, 3* and *4.* Only then does Paul turn his attention to holy living, in chapter five.

In their manner of interpretation the automatic-sanctification teachers range from the careless to the bizarre. They seem shameless in their constant misuse of God's Word, bludgeoning it about to suit their unusual opinions and brainwaves. And they constantly use *justification* scriptures to teach *sanctification* theories.

As this matter is so important, a quick review of the first two chapters of *Galatians* must be made. In *Galatians 1.6* the apostle states clearly that his subject is – 'another gospel'. Then in *Galatians 2.4-5* the apostle mentions false brethren (Judaizers) who sneaked into the churches in order to plot against the doctrine of justification by faith alone.

In *Galatians 2.11* we note that Peter yielded to these Judaizing brethren and had to be withstood by Paul. This chapter is brimming over with the subject of justification – defending it, explaining it, insisting upon it. So *Galatians 2.20* speaks of how we must be freed from the law and *justified.* How are we made clean in the sight of God? The apostle answers – by being crucified with Christ. It is our sin, our guilt, our 'old life' which is crucified with Christ.

When, therefore, the apostle says in *Galatians 2.20,* 'Nevertheless I live; yet not I, but Christ liveth in me,' he is undoubtedly speaking about the result of justification.

Once I am justified (converted), to live is to walk with Christ. Christ now has an interest in me. His plans and purposes are now being worked out in me. I am His property. I have a new principle of life in me, with new tastes and enjoyments. I am bound for

Heaven, and none shall ever pluck me from His hand. He is ever with me, to bless, strengthen, and, if necessary, to chastise and reprove.

Galatians 2.20 is the fruit of being justified by faith. There is no intention on the part of the apostle to teach or imply a *by-faith* method of achieving holiness (which would contradict all the exhortations to effort which he proceeds to give in *Galatians 5* and *6*).

In the study of these passages we must always remember the differences between *justification* and *sanctification*. *Justification* is the matter of being pardoned and declared righteous (through Christ), whereas *sanctification* is the process of being *made* righteous. *Justification* is something which takes place once and for ever at conversion. It is a declaration by God. *Sanctification*, on the other hand, is continuous and progressive and will not be finally completed until we go to Heaven.

Justification is achieved absolutely and entirely by God alone, but *sanctification* includes the effort and application of the regenerate person.

6. *Are We to Fight Sin?*

HOW IS IT THAT many Bible-reading Christians miss the fighting language of the New Testament? Think of Paul's words in *Ephesians 6.13*: 'Wherefore take unto you the whole armour of God, that ye may be able to withstand in the evil day, and having done all, to stand.'

The first truth to be noted in this text is that *there is a battle to be fought*, and while it must be fought with the armour and weapons provided by the Lord, the battle will be fought by the believer who wears the armour and wields the sword.

In this passage there are several items of military equipment which we must personally take up and use. Every piece of the armour of God is vital. No single act (such as seeking a baptism of the Spirit) can take the place of the several duties to which the Scripture refers. All the accoutrements of spiritual warfare are needed because the devil is so subtle. Throughout the New Testament the words for sanctification are all fighting terms – *mortify*, *crucify*, *strive*, *wrestle*, and *fight*.

Another passage which helps on this subject is *Philippians 2.12-13*, where Paul says, 'Work out your own salvation with fear and trembling. For it is God which worketh in you both to will and to do of his good pleasure.'

At a casual glance there seems to be a contradiction between the two halves of this quotation. One moment the apostle tells us to work out our own salvation with fear and trembling, and the next he tells us that it is God Who works in us. But obviously the apostle would not contradict himself within a few words. He tells us, on our part, to strive for holiness and obedience, because the Spirit's method is to put within us the *will* to strive, and also the strength to succeed.

In other words the Spirit does not bypass our efforts (as the automatic-sanctification teachers imagine), but gives us the desire and determination to strive for advance. We could paraphrase Paul's words thus: 'For it is God Who works in you bringing your will to desire His way, and bringing your motives, desires and actions to be entirely aligned to His pleasure.'

We could marshal very many passages from the epistles to show that the apostle Paul always urged believers to engage *personally* and *directly* in the battle against sin. The struggle for holiness is an unavoidable experience for the believer. It cannot be bypassed or handed over to the Lord. To engage in this conflict is an absolute duty, and we are promised the ever-present help and power of the Holy Spirit.

In *Galatians 5.16-17* Paul tells us plainly about the battle which we must experience. He says, 'This I say then, Walk in the Spirit, and ye shall not fulfil the lust of the flesh. For the flesh lusteth against the Spirit, and the Spirit against the flesh: and these are contrary the one to the other: so that ye cannot do the things that ye would.'

As we might expect, Spirit-baptism writers derive from these verses a variety of meanings which one would never see without their ingenious twists of interpretation. Some say that these verses teach the hopelessness of engaging in the battle against sin! They say that taking up the fight ourselves will lead to impossible turmoil and failure, so instead we should concentrate on our communion with the Holy Spirit and with Christ, and then the Lord will look after our holiness.

Others say that these verses refer to the Holy Spirit fighting the battle for us, so that we cannot fall into sin.

But the plain sense of the passage (and the interpretation given by the overwhelming majority of Bible commentators) is as follows. Because we are Christians, our old, sinful self is in conflict with our new, Spirit-indwelt nature. If we walk spiritually, praying for help, then the battle will become *even more intense*, because the Holy Spirit will wake up our consciences so that temptations and sinful desires will cause us great pain and discomfort, making it hard for us to sin. The Holy Spirit will ring the alarm bells of conscience, but we will have a part to play in responding to these alarms.

This activity of the Spirit will often produce a great conflict within us. As soon as we proceed to yield to temptation and indulge in sin, strong pangs of conscience will hold us back. If we resent the voice of conscience, suppress its challenge, and resist its pressure, then we 'trample' not only on conscience, but also on the Spirit. If we justify our sin and stifle these spiritual instincts, then the Holy Spirit will be grieved, our hearts will grow hard and cold, our consciences may be bludgeoned into insensibility, and sin will revive within us. If, however, we respond to the challenge of conscience and cry out to God to help us, we will be strengthened to resist and defeat the temptation.

The battle within us is irksome and sometimes painful, but it is life and health to our souls. There is work for us to do in this battle, as the apostle constantly shows.

Why are there so many exhortations and commands to holiness in the Bible if it is not necessary for us to obey them?

In *Galatians 6* the first six verses contain positive, practical duties which the believer must personally carry out. These are called sowing to the Spirit *(Galatians 6.8)*. The fact is that *we* must do these things. To do them will be difficult and perhaps even exhausting, for the apostle goes on to say – 'And let us not be weary in well doing: for in due season we shall reap, if we faint not.'

In other words – the battle against sin, and the struggle to obey the Lord, cannot be avoided. May no reader be confused by any of the incredible theories and teachings about holiness proposed by Spirit-baptism teachers.

7. Must We Be Emptied or Broken?

A PARTICULARLY dangerous departure from historic, biblical Christianity is to be seen in the claim of Spirit-baptism teachers that our 'personhood' must be constantly torn out and crucified afresh in order to attain to holiness. The real *you*, they insist (even after conversion), is apparently unchanged, unhallowed and untouched by the new birth. It is all bad and it must be utterly broken and thrown away.

But the Scriptures say that God is working in us to do something far greater than that. His plan is to cause the new person to *want* and to *will* the right things.

The Bible teaches that God is working in us to progressively sanctify the heart which was renewed at conversion, not to rip it out and replace it. Grace first transforms us and then progressively refines us. The Spirit-baptism movement takes away from God His right and power to *change* Christians from glory to glory. It virtually says that nothing can alter or improve humanity – not even conversion. We can only be sanctified by being depersonalised and entirely taken over by the Spirit. If any small grain of us continues to exist, the battle will be lost. Only if we become completely empty vessels can any victory occur – that is the teaching of most Spirit-baptism, automatic-sanctification groups.

Like nearly all the ideas of these teachers, this concept is the exact opposite of what is taught in the Scriptures. There we see ourselves as *transformed* children of God, equipped by the new birth with spiritual faculties and a measure of power over sin. Certainly we continue to need the mighty power of God, and we will fall if we proceed alone. But the amazing truth is that, unworthy as we are, we *are* special, different, and already partially empowered for the fight against sin. The Word of God says:

> 'But ye are a chosen generation, a royal priesthood, an holy nation, a peculiar people; that ye should shew forth the praises of him who hath called you out of darkness into his marvellous light: which in time past were not a people, but are now the people of God: which had not obtained mercy, but now have obtained mercy' *(1 Peter 2.9-10).*

We must appreciate our wonderful 'status' as sons and members of the heavenly family. We are not saved to be zombies, puppets, or robots. We are not born again to be empty vessels. It is crucial to realise that in sanctification God deals with us as children. The Spirit-baptism system of sanctification misses this point entirely. God deals with us, according to the Scripture, as beloved and privileged sons and daughters. At conversion He has made all of us to be unique and special, and it is His will that each of His children should voluntarily strive to please and serve Him with their own born-again faculties, *plus* the mighty help of the Spirit. At conversion (the only true baptism of the Spirit) the Holy Spirit gives us a new life, with new faculties and a new nature, and this is not something to be broken as though it were utterly hopeless.

Any system of sanctification which claims that the only way to be sanctified is to be emptied and to become 'nothing at all', has completely misunderstood the glorious teaching of the Word. Yet Spirit-baptism teachers so often insist that we can only be sanctified as we renounce all effort and accept that we have no contribution to make.

God has given us many precious powers and privileges. If we tear down or disregard the transforming work which took place at conversion, and convince ourselves that we are hopeless, worthless, powerless, empty vessels, then we misunderstand and abuse what

God has done for us. Part of our sanctification is to *voluntarily* serve Him more and more, and to love Him more, and to be privileged with responsibility for Him. We are to use the new faculties which He has given us as sons and heirs, and we are to love and serve Him with all our heart, and all our soul, and all our strength, and all our mind, as the Word commands us to do.

The notions of the Spirit-baptism teachers constantly conflict with the language of God's Word. They are strange and peculiar ideas which must be avoided by Christian people.

8. The Filling of the Spirit

THERE IS AN OLD SAYING, 'One baptism; many fillings.' The biblical position, we believe, is that the only baptism of the Holy Spirit is that which occurs in connection with regeneration, at conversion. Whether we choose to call it a baptism *with* the Spirit, or a baptism *of* the Spirit, the Bible makes clear, as we have seen, that it is one and the same baptism, and it occurs at conversion. However, there is in the New Testament a further blessing by the Spirit which is called the *filling* of the Spirit, and this may happen often in the life of a Christian.

This is nothing like the additional baptism of the Spirit which Pentecostalists, charismatics and higher-life teachers say we must have after conversion. Their baptism is an ecstatic experience, usually accompanied by various physical sensations and the gift of tongues. Most of them say that through this baptism the Spirit takes over from us the work of sanctification, so that we may proceed on 'autopilot' and take no active part in the conquest of our sin. We shall have, they claim, automatic holiness.

Other teachers, as we have seen, say that this baptism is for wonderful feelings of assurance and glory and communion with God.

However, the *filling* of the Spirit, which is mentioned a number of times in *Acts*, is quite different in character and purpose from the baptism proclaimed by Pentecostalists etc. To discover the nature of this filling, we will first list eight references to it in *Acts*.

Acts 2.4. On the Day of Pentecost all the disciples were filled.

Acts 4.8. When Peter gave his defence he was filled with the Spirit.

Acts 4.31-32. The disciples were filled again with the Spirit in answer to their prayer (prayed in verse 29). They asked for, and received, great boldness. They also received a spirit of oneness and love.

Acts 6.3. The filling of the Spirit was regarded as a qualification for the first diaconate. Spiritual wisdom and holiness of life indicated this filling.

Acts 7.55. Stephen was filled with the Spirit and given grace for martyrdom.

Acts 9.17. Paul was filled following his conversion,

and thereby prepared to stand up to the things which God was about to show him (see *Acts 9.15-16*), and for his new role (vv 19-20).

Acts 13.9. The Holy Spirit filled Paul again in preparation for his work, and granted him discernment and boldness.

Acts 13.52. The disciples of Pisidian Antioch were given great joy and assurance when they were filled with the Spirit. They were strengthened to witness in a difficult place in the midst of persecution.

As we study these references we realise that the same people were sometimes present at more than one filling. They were therefore filled more than once, at different times and for different objectives.

The purpose of these fillings is clear from the circumstances of the recipients, and the effects which they had. Filling of the Spirit produced boldness, fluency in witness, great love, unity of purpose, deep commitment to the Lord's work (seen in the stewardship of all their goods), wisdom, discernment, spiritual comfort in persecution, assurance and also joy. We note that these fillings of the Spirit are usually referred to in terms of their *results*, and never in terms of how they felt.

The very earliest filling was accompanied by the great sign of speaking in real foreign languages, so that the disciples preached to Jews in the different languages of the regions from which they came. None of the other filling references include tongues-speaking, contrary to the careless claims of many writers.*

The apostle Paul also refers to the filling of the Spirit in *Ephesians 5.18* – a chapter about self-control, holiness and wise behaviour. He tells us that a filling of the Spirit is to be sought to accomplish these objectives. The filling, then, is a very practical benefit which empowers believers (in *Acts*) to witness, preach, sacrifice, steward and love, and also (in *Ephesians*) to lead a holy life.

It is surely significant that in *Acts* the filling was never asked for in name by those who received it. There is no indication that they ever prayed for it in a specific way. They certainly prayed for the power and help of God to accomplish various things (eg: *Acts 4.29*). But although they did not specifically ask for it, what they received was a filling of the Spirit.

In other words, the filling of the Spirit was not an experience which was to be sought *for its own sake.* Nor are we told in *Acts* that it involved any felt sensations of any kind. (These are invented by over-imaginative teachers.) The only *feelings* we can connect to a filling of the Spirit (from studying the *Acts* references) are those of joy and love. Doubtless also the

---

* The only two other occurrences of tongues-speaking in *Acts* (besides *Acts 2*) are in *Acts 10.46* and *Acts 19.6.* These, as we show in the appendix, were not *fillings* of the Spirit, but *outpourings,* serving as 'miniature Pentecosts'.

disciples felt strongly assured, because they received power and boldness.

There is no mention of feelings such as tingling sensations up and down the spine, or waves of heat, or ecstasies, or power, or involuntary lifting of the arms. Nothing physical is referred to or hinted at in the entire record of fillings. No one broke out in uncontrolled shouting (not even 'Hallelujah!'). No one lay prostrate on the ground weeping and calling out. Present-day charismatics and second-blessing writers claim a long list of extraordinary sensations which are not to be seen anywhere in the New Testament. In *Acts* and *Ephesians* the filling of the Spirit is always a practical empowering, and never an ecstatic experience. These fillings all have a *definite, practical result.*

Today many people seek an experience of the Spirit purely for some personal, sensational kick. They want a wonderful experience, or they want to be exempted from the battle against sin. But there is nothing like that in the Word of God. We must never seek a spiritual experience for its own sake, or as a means of 'opting out' of the struggle for holiness. The help of the Spirit is always given for a practical objective.

We note that the practical result of the filling of the Spirit was to give the disciples power to *do* something, but not to have it done for them. Every single filling in the New Testament empowered the disciples, prepared the disciples or helped the disciples – to *do* something extremely hard. There is no sign of that unscriptural catch-phrase 'Let go, let God!' in the fillings of the *Book of Acts.*

This brings us to the perfect scripture for giving balance and perspective about the Holy Spirit and His wonderful work in our hearts. It is the verse at the end of *2 Corinthians* – 'The grace of the Lord Jesus Christ, and the love of God, and the communion of the Holy Ghost, be with you all.'

The *communion* or partnership of the Holy Spirit is the amazing kindness and condescension of the Spirit whereby He 'stoops down to us and enfolds us in His communion' (the words of Bible commentator R. C. H. Lenski). It is the Holy Spirit Who imparts to us the blessings of our salvation, bringing us into the family of the redeemed. Whatever Christ has secured for us, the Holy Spirit applies to our lives, and through Him we become sharers; partners of spiritual life itself.

But the word *communion* or partnership includes a vital principle which automatic-sanctification teachers (such as Andrew Murray and Watchman Nee) entirely pass by. This school of writers teaches that unless the Holy Spirit possesses and fills every part and crevice of our being (leaving absolutely nothing of *us*) we cannot possibly be truly sanctified. We have seen already that by this theory of sanctification the Lord really accomplishes nothing at all in the lives of His people, who become mere empty shells, the Spirit Himself substituting for, rather than refining, their faculties. There is no *sharing*, no *partnership* at all, only disposal of personhood, and take-over.

The correct concept is that God's amazing grace takes vile sinners, converts them, and then gradually makes them saints. This can be accomplished because the Holy Spirit shares Himself with us. He is the gentle Holy Spirit Who works on behalf of Christ, of Whom it was prophesied, 'a bruised reed shall he not break, and the smoking flax shall he not quench.'

The Holy Spirit does not smash us and take us over. He imparts His life into ours and brings us to share the things of the eternal Godhead. He does not eclipse us, and take away all our identity and responsibility. He comes alongside to enrich and empower us. He is a *partner*, even in the business sense of the word.

A person may dream of running a small business, a shop perhaps, but may not have the necessary money. If he is fortunate, a wealthy partner may provide the capital. There would be no business without the capital, but the wealthy partner who provides it does not become involved in the day-to-day labour of the business. He does not arrive in the morning to open the shop, remove the shutters, put out the goods, or operate the cash till. The *active* partner does all these things, while the sponsor provides the capital.

The illustration is far from perfect, but the Holy Spirit is a *partner* to us. Whenever more 'capital' is needed, we turn to our infinitely rich and powerful partner, for we are entirely dependent upon Him for wherewithal and counsel. The relationship is a *partnership.*

When the apostle Paul prays that the *communion,* or *sharing* or *partnership* of the Holy Ghost may be with us all, he reminds us that we depend on the Holy Spirit for our power, and yet he also reminds us that there is much for us to do in the pursuit of sanctification.

Numerous charismatic and higher-life authors claim that *Ephesians 5.18* proves that it is necessary for our own identity to be displaced in every respect by the occupation of the Spirit – 'And be not drunk with wine, wherein is excess; but be filled with the Spirit.' Does this verse really tell us that to receive the fulness of the Spirit we must totally empty ourselves, and look to the Holy Spirit to do everything for us?

The Greek *filling* word is used many times in the New Testament. It is used, for example, in *Romans 11.25,* where Paul speaks of the 'fulness of the gentiles' having come in. Does this imply that all those Jews (and some gentiles) who had already been saved during Old Testament times, would all be evacuated and jettisoned to make way for the gentiles? Of course not. The *filling up* word as used here does not mean that the Lord disposed of every single Jew and started again. Similarly, when the apostle speaks of the *fulness* of Israel *(Romans 11.12)* he refers to the complete number of the redeemed being made up. He means *completion*, not emptying and filling.

In *Romans 15.14* the apostle Paul commends the Romans for being 'filled with all knowledge'. Did he mean that they had cast out of their minds everything they ever knew, and taken in entirely new knowledge? Of course not. He rejoiced because their secular knowledge had now been massively added to and *crowned* by spiritual knowledge. Equally, he did not mean that they now knew everything. The filling word does not always imply either complete evacuation, or absolute fulness.

A similar reference is found in *Ephesians 3.19*, where the apostle prays that they might be 'filled with all the fulness of God'. This, of course, is impossible. Reading these words we do not for a moment think that the Ephesians could be completely filled with all the infinite being of Almighty God.

We must understand the words *filled* and *filling* in a less than fully literal way. The original Greek word simply means to *fill up* or *complete*, and sometimes it means to *add* or *top up*. Various lexicons give its meaning as – *to complete, to replete, to cram, to level up, to fully furnish, to finish.*

If we fill a water jug, it does not necessarily mean that we throw away the water already in the jug. We simply fill it up. The *filling* of the Spirit does not totally scrap the individual person or displace him. The Spirit makes up our deficiencies. He gives power where we are weak, wisdom where we are ignorant or naive, courage where we are cowardly, and in many other ways also He makes up our deficiencies.

So the exhortation to pray always for the filling of the Spirit (given in *Ephesians 5.18*) is completely consistent with that final verse in *2 Corinthians*, which spoke of the Holy Spirit as being in communion or in partnership with us. *We* strive for holiness, and *He* blesses with power.

The aim of the Spirit is to build something worthwhile in *our* lives, not to entirely replace our faculties with His own glorious presence and power. The goal is not to be emptied of all personal capacities so as to become hopeless and pathetic. Conversion has bestowed upon us a range of gifts, strengths and abilities, and these are to be dedicated to God and exercised, not neglected or discarded.

The filling of the Spirit is the invisible and usually unfelt empowering of the Spirit which strengthens and enables us whenever we sincerely and humbly cry out to God for help.

We must begin every day by recognising our need of help for holiness, for witness and for the Lord's service. And as we do so, and pray to God for strength, fluency and boldness, we will receive a further filling or preparation by the Spirit of God.

9. The Spirit's Way

THE HOLY SPIRIT does not sanctify by a special baptism, or by taking over the battle, but by convicting and stirring the hearts of believers, and then by strengthening them. This work of sanctification begins from the time of conversion – the occurrence of the one and only *baptism* of the Spirit – and is carried out through a range of means. Some of the Spirit's ways are set out in this chapter, though the order is not intended to reflect any scale of importance.

1. Faith

First, the Holy Spirit sanctifies by *our faith*, for we read in *Ephesians 6.16*: 'Above all, taking the shield of faith, wherewith ye shall be able to quench all the fiery darts *[temptations]* of the wicked.' Obviously, this does not mean that we are sanctified by faith in the sense that the Spirit-baptism teachers claim. Our faith helps us in sanctification because, as we exercise faith and trust in the power and promises of God, we become –

(a) more ready to give ourselves to His commands and His service, and

(b) more able to face up to the knocks and trials of life.

When we really believe that our sovereign God is watching over us, we naturally behave better, and we are also helped to endure sufferings and set-backs without self-pity, bitterness, jealousy, spite and so on. While we keep a strong trust in our Saviour, and keep His promises in view, we also avoid falling into the slough of despond.

When the allurements of this passing world begin to get some hold upon us, and we are tempted to desire worldly things, or to yield to worldly flattery or ambitions, then our faith and trust in God's plan and purpose will hold us safe. We shall remember that this is a vain and fallen world which can never be trusted, and the saying of *1 John 5.4* will be fulfilled in our experience – 'For whatsoever is born of God overcometh the world: and this is the victory that overcometh the world, even our faith.'

On another front, our faith is the shield which protects us from the lies which the devil whispers to us in his campaign to steal our assurance and our joy and peace.

Faith enables us to live as people who owe a great debt to the Saviour. As we remember our wonderful deliverance from sin and death, and the amazing blessings which are ours, we become ashamed of our sinfulness, and we reason in the same way as Paul, who said, 'We are debtors, not to the flesh, to live after the flesh . . . For I reckon that the sufferings of this present time are not worthy to be compared with the glory which shall be revealed in us' *(Romans 8.12* and *18)*.

Faith, hope and love go together, and when we keep our faith bright and sincere, we are also full of gratitude and love for the Lord. We gladly set our affections on things above, not on things on the earth *(Colossians 3.2)*, and we are spurred to conscientious effort to please the Lord by godly living.

Where does our faith come from? It comes obviously from the Holy Spirit, Who imparted it to us at conversion – the only baptism of the Spirit.

2. The Word of God

A second principal method of producing advance in sanctification, by the Spirit, is the *right use of the Word of God.* Every believer is familiar with Paul's words in *2 Timothy 3.16*: 'All scripture is given by inspiration of God, and is profitable for doctrine, for reproof, for correction, for instruction in righteousness.'

God's Word will sometimes *reprove* us so that we have to put matters right, either in our lives, or in our church conduct. It will *correct* us, so that we modify our ways when we have drifted off course. It will *instruct* us, so that we become equipped to carry out every good work. We must allow the Scriptures to challenge us.

We note that Timothy is told that in preaching this Word he should 'reprove, rebuke, exhort with all longsuffering and doctrine' *(2 Timothy 4.2)*. The pulpit is to apply the Word of God, so that it speaks very strongly to the conduct, habits and errors of believers. Through the Word, whether read or preached, we fulfil the desire of the Lord as expressed in His prayer for His people *(John 17.17)* – 'Sanctify them through thy truth: thy word is truth.'

The Word of God is obviously a chief means of sanctification as it challenges, provokes and exhorts the people of God. But do we have the right level of awe and respect for the Word to respond to it? Too many people talk much about their baptism of the Spirit, and about their ecstasies and words of knowledge and so on, but they fail to obey even the basic commands of God's authoritative Word. What kind of Spirit-baptism is that?

The promoters of Spirit-baptism around the world are the most notorious teachers for ignoring the rules and standards of God's Word. We see this in their worldliness: their love of worldly pleasures and type of music, and the way they pervert worship to these tastes.

True spiritual life and obedience is to be seen in a person's love, awe and reverence for the Word, and obedience to its teaching.

3. Special dedication

A third route to sanctification is to be seen in *special acts of commitment or dedication.* We could refer to a large number of scriptures to establish the great value of acts of special dedication, but perhaps the most obvious is *Romans 12.* In verse 1 Paul writes: 'I beseech you therefore, brethren, by the mercies of God, that ye present your bodies a living sacrifice, holy, acceptable unto God, which is your reasonable service.'

It may be said that this is a standard for Christians all the time, and this is certainly true. But Paul calls us to renew our vows in a special act of dedication, and in his exhortation he uses the language of an act of sacrifice.

We are not just to drift along in the Christian life, with only general and vague aspirations to be more committed to the Lord. From time to time we are to take ourselves in hand and make a definite commitment of ourselves. We are to review every department of our activity, and then give ourselves up to the Lord, together with our time, energy and resources; indeed, everything we are and have.

An act of dedication may take a negative form, as when the children of Israel were told to keep apart from 'the accursed thing' *(Joshua 6.18)*. But Achan disobeyed and took the forbidden spoil, bringing disaster to his family. Holiness involves obedience to God in remaining apart from things which God condemns.

The well-known words of *2 Corinthians 6.17* command separation from unrighteousness and idolatry – 'Wherefore come out from among them, and be ye separate, saith the Lord, and touch not the unclean thing; and I will receive you.' We are to have nothing to do with evil, or with worldliness, or with false religious teachers, who spurn the infallible Word of God, and teach error in the name of Christ. Our love for the Lord and for His Word should lead us to obey God's call.

Amazingly, those who claim super-spiritual baptisms are among the most *un*separated and disobedient people claiming the name of Christ! Throughout the world the vast majority of charismatic leaders are in close alliance with apostate denominations and false teachers. Very many advocate unity of Bible believers with non-Bible believers. Their ultimate goal and desire is one world-wide church headed by the pope! How can they possibly be 'baptised' and 'filled' with the Holy Spirit, when He, in the Word, commands that His born-again people must never join themselves with error?

We repeat the sad fact that many who claim to have received a special baptism of the Spirit live extremely worldly lives. The overwhelming majority of so-called Christian rock bands and choirs are associated with charismatic and similar churches where there appears to be little interest in *obeying* God in these matters. The grand claims that they have a special blessing of the Spirit hardly ring true!

When the Spirit is really moving within us, we dedicate ourselves to God both positively and negatively, and keep apart from the things the Lord opposes.

4. Mortifying of sin

A fourth (but undoubtedly the main) method of sanctification, is that of mortifying or *putting to death* our sinful ways by the help of the Spirit. The principal scriptures in which we are exhorted to put to death the deeds of the body, or to 'deny' them or 'cleanse' them, are: *Romans 8.13; Colossians 3.5; Romans 6.12-13; 2 Corinthians 7.1;* and *Titus 2.11-12.* The first two of these passages read as follows:–

> 'For if ye live after the flesh, ye shall die: but if ye through the Spirit do mortify the deeds of the body, ye shall live.'
>
> 'Mortify therefore your members which are upon the earth; fornication, uncleanness, inordinate

affection, evil concupiscence, and covetousness . . .'

What is sanctification? It is the activity of personally putting to death, contradicting or rejecting the sinful desires of the body and the temptations of the devil, together with the lifestyles, fashions and allurements of the world.

Mortifying the deeds of the body is an act which we must carry out. It is something for us to do, praying to the Lord for His powerful help.

In sanctification, our wills become dedicated to this task, so that we live throughout our lives in thoughtful, intelligent, active opposition to worldly lusts. We put up a battle, an opposition, a constant resistance to the desires of the flesh.

As Paul tells us in *Romans 6.12-13*, sanctification is a matter of refusing to allow our bodily faculties, passions and parts to serve sin, and instead, consciously yielding them to do righteous deeds. In the light of such strong texts, all ideas of automatic-sanctification, or of handing the battle over to the Lord and doing nothing, are foolish, cult-like notions.*

5. Chastening of the Lord

A fifth means of our sanctification is the *chastening of the Lord.* This is clearly taught in *Hebrews 12.5-6*

---

*A fuller explanation of this aspect of sanctification is provided in a booklet by Dr Masters entitled *Eight Steps to Avoid Sin* (Sword & Trowel, London).

where the writer says: 'My son, despise not thou the chastening of the Lord, nor faint when thou art rebuked of him: for whom the Lord loveth he chasteneth, and scourgeth every son whom he receiveth.' We are not to despise this chastening, which is a recurring process in our lives.

We see in these verses a twofold discipline – the *chastening* and the *rebuke*. The *chastening* is the more gentle of the two, because we are sometimes inclined to 'despise' it, or disregard it. The *rebuke* is obviously much more severe, because when it comes we are inclined to 'faint'. So we see a carefully directed, fatherly discipline bringing us to our senses when we go wrong.

An even more severe form of discipline is seen in *1 Corinthians 11.30*: 'For this cause many are weak and sickly among you, and many sleep.' Some believers have had to be very severely judged because of their unspiritual behaviour in the matter of fellowship relationships, and their lack of self-examination. They have not shown any concern to lead sanctified lives, and God has had to punish them. The apostle says, 'For if we would judge ourselves, we should not be judged.'

The significant point about chastening is that it is a process of love, from the Father to His child. 'God dealeth with you as with sons,' says *Hebrews 12.7*; 'for what son is he whom the father chasteneth not?' The

Lord has an ongoing programme of infinitely wise (and no doubt as gentle as possible) chastisement for the training of His children when they stray from the mark. It is not enjoyable (contrary to the 'happy-all-the-day' ideas of Spirit-baptism teachers), but it leads to peace and righteousness to 'them which are exercised' by it *(Hebrews 12.11)*. It is the indwelling Holy Spirit's work to bring us to the point where we eventually respond meekly, rather than bitterly, to such chastisement.

6. Sickness and Suffering

A sixth means of bringing about our sanctification is by *experiences of suffering and sickness.* These are *not* only given to chastise, but also to train and develop our patience and faith. The Lord may use sickness and suffering to chastise, as we have just noted, but equally He uses such trials for our positive development.

While the Lord may heal in answer to prayer, it may be that a believer is called to endure a period of sickness, and through this the Lord will deepen prayer and spiritual knowledge and experience. Paul testifies to this in *2 Corinthians 12.9* where he tells us that God declined to heal him, saying, 'My grace is sufficient for thee: for my strength is made perfect in weakness.' Paul's response was, 'Most gladly therefore will I rather glory in my infirmities, that the power of Christ may rest upon me.'

Trials also contribute to our witness, for others see that we have a very real grip on divine help, and a wonderful source of comfort and joy.

There are many benefits and purposes to sickness, and sanctification is certainly one of them. Such trials lead God's people to self-examination and review of their lives; cause them to consider their frailty and dependence upon God's power; and stir them to think of the future, and to review their commitment to the Lord's service. Trials obviously give time for prayer, communion, and intercession for others.

In sickness, souls become more important than bodies, Heaven more important than earth, and bringing pleasure to the Lord more important than pleasing self.

In sickness believers often gain higher and deeper views of the Lord than at any other time, grasping more of His omnipotence and infinite holiness.

How often it has been said that sickness is the believer's second-best blessing after health, and so it should be, for 'all things work together for good to them that love God' *(Romans 8.28)*.

What is it that makes sickness a lighthouse of Truth and a fountain of pleasure to a believer, when it is all horror to an unbeliever? Is it a special baptism of the Spirit? No, it is the work of the mighty, loving Holy Spirit Who dwells within every true believer from the time of conversion. By *His* grace and goodness, we may walk through the very darkest valleys of life's journey, so that they become places of spiritual experience and advance.

7. Mutual admonition

A seventh means of our sanctification is the *practice of mutual admonition* among the Lord's people. Four scriptures (out of many) may be quoted to prove this duty – *Romans 15.14, Colossians 3.16, Galatians 6.1* and *James 5.19-20*:

'And I myself also am persuaded of you, my brethren, that ye also are full of goodness, filled with all knowledge, able also to admonish one another.'

'Let the word of Christ dwell in you richly in all wisdom; teaching and admonishing one another.'

'Brethren, if a man be overtaken in a fault, ye which are spiritual, restore such an one in the spirit of meekness; considering thyself, lest thou also be tempted.'

'Brethren, if any of you do err from the truth, and one convert him; let him know, that he which converteth the sinner from the error of his way shall save a soul from death, and shall hide a multitude of sins.'

The ministry of mutual admonition is of incalculable value, but it is an activity which is possible only where believers are truly close to each other in spiritual oneness and friendship, and where they are able to admonish with true humility and grace. The Lord will certainly use us to contribute to one another's progress in sanctification. This is another method of sanctification not included in the ideas of the advocates of Spirit-baptism and automatic-sanctification. The fact is, however, that the Lord sets believers in families (churches), and the Spirit, Who indwells them from conversion, uses them to minister to one another by encouragement, warning and friendly exhortation.

Conclusion

These seven routes or ways by which the Spirit sanctifies depend upon His superintendency of our circumstances, and His silent work in our hearts. It is the Holy Spirit Who makes us receptive to various correcting, shaping influences. He works in such a way that we freely, willingly and personally strive to advance, praying for His help.

10. A Baptism of Bliss?

MANY ADVOCATES OF a post-conversion baptism of the Spirit insist that Spirit-filled Christians are not only automatically made holy, but are also continuously happy and even healthy. They promise an uninterrupted enjoyment of the power and presence of Christ as long as the believer 'abides in Christ' and 'walks in the Spirit'.

The classic example of this idea is to be seen in *How to Live the Victorious Life* – the anonymous best seller which has presented this point of view over several decades. The person experiencing the baptism and fulness of the Spirit has, it is claimed, a most wonderful life.

'It is a life of perfect rest. All unrest dishonours Christ. It is a life of perfect peace. To experience

> anything but peace – even under opposition, oppression, loss, bereavement, or perplexity – is to dishonour Christ and His Word. It is a life lived by the Christ dwelling in us, and therefore a life of perfect joy. Such a life is a victorious life – a life of constant miracle.'

A more modern best seller, *The Holy Spirit and You*, by Dennis and Rita Bennett (founders, with others, of the charismatic movement in America in the 1960s), includes health in the bliss of the Christian:–

> 'The Scriptures promise health for the believer . . . if we become ill, God will heal us. People say: "You're not going to live for ever. You've got to die sometime!" True. But long life is promised to God's people, and when we do go home to our Father, it is not necessary that we go in disease and pain.'

Suffering, to these teachers, is merely God's way of breaking down our reliance on self, and leading us to a total dependence upon Himself. Once this higher ground is attained, spiritual and physical trials and setbacks come to an end. Should any believer experience sadness, failure or loss of elevated feeling and assurance, it will be blamed on a failure of faith having allowed the flesh to reassert control.

These teachers unwittingly consign the apostles to the ranks of faithless, carnal Christians, not to mention the heroes of church history such as reformers and revival instruments. All these experienced tremendous suffering and constant set-backs. Spirit-baptism teachers create images of spiritual experience which are unbiblical, unreal and highly emotional. They deny the Lord His right to draw the clouds across the heavens so that our warmer spiritual feelings are temporarily eclipsed. Scripture, however, teaches that these moments are the Lord's way of drawing out our deepest reserves of trust and love.

There are countless earnest believers who have been trained by Spirit-baptism teachers to equate spirituality with a kind of emotional 'high', or 'cloud nine' experience, and they have been made to live in a self-induced mood of religious excitement and joy.

Such a shallow view of suffering simply takes no account of the plain teaching of so much Scripture. Did not the Lord Jesus Christ, our perfect forerunner and example, experience suffering throughout His life? Was He not (even prior to Calvary) a 'man of sorrows, and acquainted with grief'? Yet our Saviour was the perfect man. He suffered reproach and heaviness but all without sin. It would be blasphemous to suggest that our Lord's life was anything but perfect and holy, or that His communion with the Father was ever clouded.

The apostles also knew great trials. Paul speaks of being troubled on every side, perplexed and persecuted. He tells us he was constantly delivered unto death for Jesus' sake. He speaks of having much tribulation, and no rest, with 'fightings without', and 'fears within'. He owns to being cast down, and he suffered the continual distress of the thorn in his flesh. He mentions infirmities, reproaches, necessities, persecutions, distresses and weakness. For his countrymen he had great heaviness and continual sorrow in his heart.* Was the apostle unspiritual in these feelings?

In that famous chapter, *Romans 8,* Paul says that we know that all things work together for our good, and that we may be more than conquerors, even though we feel the pain of suffering (v 18), and also of many other woes including nakedness, peril, sword and slaughter (vv 35-39).

This is a deep subject which we cannot fully expound in this study, but true sanctification does not immunise us from troubles and distresses. It enables us to live through them according to the promise of *Isaiah 43.2* – 'When thou passest through the waters, I will be with thee; and through the rivers, they shall not overflow thee: when thou walkest through the fire, thou shalt not be burned; neither shall the flame kindle upon thee.'

There can be no credibility in any view of Spirit-baptism or of sanctification which takes no account of the place of suffering in the life of a believer. We cannot and must not respect a system which fails to

---

*See *2 Corinthians 4.8-9; 7.5; 12.7-10; Romans 9.1-3.*

acknowledge that part of our training in this life is to learn to trust the Lord in times of darkness and trial.

The same is true of bodily sickness. Although the apostle Paul could not heal Trophimus or Timothy (and gave the latter practical advice rather than healing), some Spirit-baptism writers insist that bodily sickness is not meant to persist in a believer. It is, they claim, either a punishment from God, or it is due to the believer's failure in seeking the fulness of the Spirit and the healing which this will bring. However, Scripture commends patient suffering in affliction and illness. While God may hear our prayers for healing, He may equally call us to prove Him and witness to Him in and through suffering.*

It is of very great importance that we realise that the teachings of charismatic and other Spirit-baptism groups stand in complete opposition to 'traditional' evangelical doctrine. They are not merely slightly different, but are a point-by-point contradiction of all the principles of Scripture on holiness, healing and assurance. When concerned believers really begin to study the texts, they invariably come to see how wide of the mark the new ideas are, and how sure and glorious are the time-honoured doctrines.

---

* See Dr Masters' book, *The Healing Epidemic* (Wakeman Trust, London), for a full treatment of divine healing.

APPENDIX

The Case of the Ephesus Twelve

And it came to pass, that, while Apollos was at Corinth, Paul having passed through the upper coasts came to Ephesus: and finding certain disciples, he said unto them, Have ye received the Holy Ghost since ye believed? And they said unto him, We have not so much as heard whether there be any Holy Ghost (Acts 19.1-2).

WE HAVE OBSERVED that the *Acts* passage quoted here is a favourite proof text among Spirit-baptism teachers for the necessity of a baptism of the Spirit in addition to conversion, coupled with the gift of tongues.

Does Paul's action of laying his hands on the men to impart the Holy Spirit justify these ideas? The answer is no, and the correct explanation of the event is as follows.

The men Paul met in the synagogue were described by Luke as *disciples*, a term which he generally reserved for believers. It turned out that they had been baptised by disciples of John the Baptist, which tells us that they were undoubtedly Jews. (They were obviously not the same people who are mentioned in *Acts 18.26-27.* A number of believers appear to have been associated with Aquila and Priscilla at Ephesus, but when Paul returned to the city he stumbled across this further little group.)

Paul wanted to know whether these men had experienced the Holy Spirit at the time they believed in Christ. But why did he ask this question? After all, Paul taught that *every* Christian received the Spirit automatically at the time of conversion. He stated emphatically that if any man did not have the Spirit of Christ, he was not a true Christian *(Romans 8.9).*

Why, then, should Paul have given these men the scope *not* to have received the Spirit at the time they first believed in Christ? The explanation is that Paul suspected (rightly, as it turned out) that they had come to believe in Christ through the teaching of disciples of John the Baptist. In this case they would not have known a major part of the Gospel message, nor anything about the Holy Spirit.

John had taught that Jesus was the promised Messiah Who would take away sin. He also preached the need for sincere repentance before God. John, however, died before the Lord went to Calvary, and many of his disciples migrated to various regions, teaching his message. Obviously this soon became out of date, because these migrant disciples knew nothing about Calvary, or the resurrection, or the coming of the Holy Spirit, or the founding of a separate New Testament church. Nor did they know that the Lord was now giving the New Testament Scriptures by revelation through apostles and prophets. People who heard the preaching of John's disciples received only a part of the Gospel message.

This was the problem with Apollos *(Acts 18.24-26)*. Such people experienced genuine conviction of sin, repented before God, and put their trust in Christ as the One Who would somehow take away the sin of the world, though they were not sure how. If they had heard of His crucifixion and resurrection, they certainly knew nothing of the outpouring of the Spirit. They were very likely to have been born again, but much light was missing. Most of them were believers in a 'pre-Calvary' Messiah, and they were stuck, so to speak, between the Testaments.

When Paul found the twelve disciples at Ephesus (perhaps holding their own prayer group in a corner of the synagogue) he recognised their sincerity and found that they relied upon Jesus as Messiah. But he was clearly puzzled by them. Where had they heard the Gospel? How had they been converted? Were they 'pre-Calvary' believers in the Messiah? Did they understand that the New Testament church was now quite distinct from the Jewish church? Had they, perhaps, heard the preaching of an apostle? Did they know about the new revelation being given through apostles authenticated by signs and wonders? Did they know about the coming of the Holy Spirit at Pentecost?

Had they, perhaps, like the converts in Samaria, or like the gentiles who gathered in the house of Cornelius, witnessed a local repetition of the outpouring of the Spirit (a kind of 'mini-Pentecost') given in the presence of an apostle?

Paul's concern was to find out just what these men (who appeared to have no contact with other believers) knew about all these things. So he asked his question, which we expand for clarity, 'Did you have any knowledge or experience of the Holy Spirit when or since you heard and believed the message of Christ?'

Their reply fully justified Paul's puzzlement over them. They looked at him in amazement and said, 'We have not so much as heard whether there be any Holy Spirit!'

This reply told Paul all he needed to know. He realised that although they were believers in Jesus as the Messiah, they had no idea that the promised Holy Spirit *had come*, and that the age of the New Testament church had started. He now knew that these pious souls had never come into contact with any mainstream Christian preachers, so he naturally asked them, 'Unto what then were ye baptised?' They replied, 'Unto John's baptism.' All Paul's suspicions about them were completely confirmed.

To take this passage, as some writers do, and to regard these Ephesian disciples as if they were 'fully-fledged' converts of Christian preachers, who nevertheless needed an extra baptism of the Spirit, is a very superficial interpretation. These men were caught in the gap between the Old and New Testaments. While they were genuine believers, accepted by God, they did not enjoy full Gospel light.

They knew nothing of Calvary, the resurrection, or of Pentecost until Paul explained all these things to them. Then they were baptised in the name of the Lord Jesus. Then these unusual and atypical believers were granted a remarkable blessing – an outpouring of the Holy Spirit with the gifts of tongues and prophecy. In other words, they enjoyed a miniature reproduction of the Day of Pentecost.

Why should God have granted this unusual outpouring of spiritual gifts to these dozen men? Why would He grant a 'mini-Pentecost' some 23 years after that great event? The most probable answer is that the Gospel was about to make great inroads into an entirely new and vast area. Each miniature Pentecost had an important message. The outpouring upon the Samaritan converts (recorded in *Acts 8*) was significant because it communicated a vital message both to Jewish Christians and to the Samaritan converts. Through this event Jewish believers were commanded to accept the Samaritans as true Christians, equal to themselves, and fully grafted into the Church. And the Samaritans (always frostily independent of Jerusalem) were told to obey the apostles, and recognise one spiritual family, for there was now *one* Church for all converts. (We note that there is no mention of tongues-speaking in Samaria, but the outpouring of the Spirit still ranks as a 'mini-Pentecost'.)

The outpouring of the Spirit at the house of Cornelius (recorded in *Acts 10*) again communicated an important message to two parties. Jewish Christians were emphatically told by God that the gentiles were accepted into the Church, while the gentiles were fully assured of *their* standing before God.

The meeting of Paul with the twelve 'Johnites' at Ephesus counts as the third and final recorded 'mini-Pentecost', and like the other two it had a special purpose. This purpose may be gleaned from what followed. We read in *Acts 19.8-10* of how Paul preached for two years in Ephesus, and how people throughout Asia heard the Word. Luke goes on to record how Paul (as an apostle) was personally authenticated by being given the power to work miraculous healings.

We can surely see the Lord's purpose here. There were very many Jews scattered around in those parts, and we do not forget the massive Jewish prejudice against gentiles and against the new Church order. Even tender-hearted, believing Jews thought, 'Moses can never pass away! God has told us not to swerve in the slightest from the law of Moses! We must protect it and not let anyone add to it or take away from it. But this Christian Church is all so new and so radical. These preachers are saying that our worship must change, and that the ceremonial is of no use. How can this be?'

It was in answer to these misgivings that the signs of Pentecost – designed to rebuke unbelieving Jews and to encourage those who gave up Judaism for Christ – were manifested in this vast, new region of outreach. Thus the Lord gave fresh tokens of Pentecost to liberate the Jewish conscience and to authenticate His messengers.

Perhaps no one in Ephesus beside these twelve men ever received the foreign-language gifts. There is no record that others did. The healing gifts appear to have been given only to Paul *(Acts 19.11-12)*. Tongues are not mentioned in Paul's letter to the Ephesians written later, in about 60 AD. Nevertheless, for the dozen or so men who formed the foundation of the new, regional church, God set His seal upon the authenticity of their church and mission in a remarkable way, and at the same time confirmed to any other Jewish believers that they must move on to the Church of Jesus Christ.

This leads us to the second idea which charismatic teachers derive from this event at Ephesus, namely, that in those days every believer who received the Spirit automatically spoke in tongues as evidence of having done so.

This idea, however, does not tally with the record of *Acts* which shows that few people actually received the *outward* gifts and tokens of the Spirit when He was poured out. On the Day of Pentecost a maximum of 120 people spoke in tongues *(Acts 1.15* and *2.4)*. As we noted earlier, there is no mention of the 3,000 converts doing so, even though we are given considerable detail about the evidences of their new-found spiritual life. Possibly not *all* the 120 disciples spoke in tongues, for only the *men* seem to have been heard *(Acts 2.13)*. We must remember, also, that these tongues were real languages, understood by those who came from many different countries.

The vast number of additional people whose conversions are recorded in *Acts 4* did not speak in tongues. It is clear that as far as the biblical record is concerned, therefore, only a tiny minority of people spoke in tongues around the time of Pentecost. Statistically, the highest figure, if we adhere closely to the record, is below 2.5%.

In other words, while the promised gift of the Holy Spirit *Himself* was given to every convert upon repentance *(Acts 2.38)*, yet the *outward sign-gifts* of the Spirit, which visibly authenticated His presence in the newly-formed Church, were given only to a few select people, apparently all of these being men.

Furthermore, after the time of Pentecost there seems to have been a long period of silence as far as tongues-speaking is concerned. Signs and wonders certainly went on, by the hands of apostles, but tongues-speaking does not appear to have continued on a regular basis. The evidence for this is in *Acts* chapters 10 and 11, which describe events which took place at least six years after Pentecost. (This is the shortest estimate offered by conservative scholars. Some go as high as 13 years.) Tongues are seen again for the first time after all these years, and Peter appears to say that there had been no tongues-speaking during the intervening period.

In *Acts 10* we are told about the wonderful conversion of gentiles gathered with Cornelius to listen to the preaching of Peter. As Peter was preaching, the Holy Spirit fell upon the gathered company, and they spoke in tongues, to the astonishment of the Jews who were with Peter. When Peter later recounted this to the gathered church members at Jerusalem, he expressed himself in a highly significant way, saying – 'And as I began to speak, the Holy Ghost fell on them, as on us *at the beginning' (Acts 11.15).*

Peter did not say that the Holy Ghost gave tongues, just as He did every week in the church at Jerusalem.

He referred everyone back to that remarkable phenomenon of Pentecost at least six years before. So unusual was this event, that it jarred Peter's mind so that he remembered the words of Christ – 'John indeed baptised with water; but ye shall be baptised with the Holy Ghost.' These words were taken by Peter as a reference to the general baptism of the Spirit poured out at Pentecost, and by quoting them he tells us how he viewed the event in the house of Cornelius. He saw it as a special event on a par with Pentecost, but obviously on a very much smaller scale. Nevertheless, it was a special event with a message. The message in this case was to the Jews, who needed to be convinced that believing gentiles were fully-fledged members of the Church of Jesus Christ.

The conversion of the gentiles in the house of Cornelius took place between 6 and 13 years after Pentecost, and the Ephesus incident of tongues-speaking occurred 23 years after Pentecost – around 53 or 54 AD. But there is no mention in the Scriptures of tongues-speaking taking place between the Cornelius incident and this occurrence at Ephesus, apart from the information we are given in *1 Corinthians 12-14*, where the apostle authorises a maximum of three people to contribute a message by tongues in a service as a sign-message to cynical Jews.

From these few references to tongues we discover that they were a miraculous gift of foreign-language prophecies given by God to shock and convince Jews. This purpose prevails in all three of the 'mini-Pentecost' outpourings.

Clearly, then, every believer in New Testament times did not speak in tongues or prophesy. And none received a second-blessing type of experience of the Holy Spirit. The miniature repetitions of Pentecost, three in number (and only two including tongues-speaking), were each given for special reasons, and were never intended as a picture of *normal* church life in the ongoing Church age.

Other Wakeman books by Dr Masters
dealing with aspects of the work of the Spirit

The Charismatic Phenomenon
Peter Masters & John C. Whitcomb
113 pages, paperback, ISBN 1 870855 01 9

Dr Masters, and Dr Whitcomb (co-author of the renowned work – *The Genesis Flood*), together trace the purpose of the sign-miracles and revelatory gifts of New Testament times, and their precise nature. Were they intended to be ongoing in the life of the Church? Numerous questions are here answered, such as, 'What exactly are the greater works of *John 14.12*?' and 'Are the signs following, referred to in *Mark 16*, for today?' This easy-to-read work has been helpful to many thousands having passed through six printings in an earlier edition, and three in this present edition (not to mention many translations into other languages).

The Healing Epidemic
Peter Masters
227 pages, paperback, ISBN 1 870855 00 0

The *Healing Epidemic*, now in its fourth major printing, was commended by the renowned American literary review *Bibliotheca Sacra* as – 'one of the best books on this subject today. It should be widely read by concerned Christian people of all theological persuasions.'

The author first traces the origins of the current upsurge of healing ministries. He then takes each of the eleven main arguments used by healers in support of their methods, and shows the mistaken nature of each one. He provides important facts about demonology, showing just what demons can and cannot do. He proves from Scripture that the *sign*-gifts have ceased, and tells how *James 5* should be implemented in our churches today. He also presents the biblical commands that the conscious mind should always be alert and rational for all worship and spiritual service. The book includes an assessment of miraculous healing by a leading British medical specialist, Prof Verna Wright of Leeds University Medical School.

Biblical Strategies for Witness

Peter Masters

154 pages, paperback, ISBN 1 870855 18 3

'Perhaps it is not realised,' writes Dr Masters, 'just how much detailed and practical guidance is stored in the Gospels and the *Book of Acts* for all who engage in personal witness and preaching. Are we aware, for example, that the Lord Jesus Christ employed distinctive strategies for different kinds of unbeliever, and that these may be studied and copied? In addition, the Lord regularly employed several "techniques" for opening the minds of all listeners.'

Two chapters of this book focus upon the nature of the work of the Spirit in the soul in regeneration and conversion, distinguishing between the two, and showing the genuine instrumentality of persuasive Gospel pleading.

The Baptist Confession of Faith of 1689

Updated with notes by Dr Peter Masters

91 pages, paperback, ISBN 1 870855 02 7

C. H. Spurgeon declared of this great *Confession* – 'Here the youngest members of our church will have a body of Truth in small compass, and by means of the scriptural proofs, will be able to give a reason of the hope that is in them.'

This brilliant summary of doctrine (in the same family as the *Westminster Confession*), with its invaluable proof texts, has been gently updated in punctuation, and archaic words replaced. Helpful explanations of difficult phrases have been added in italic brackets. A brief history of the *Confession*, with an index, is included.

[Compiled by the leading divines among British Baptists in the 17th century and adopted by two assemblies of Baptist churches in 1677 and 1689.]